Bias-Free Stress Measurement

ISBN 1-58961-053-9

Published by PageFree Publishing, Inc.
733 Howard Street
Otsego, Michigan 49078
616-692-3386
www.pagefreepublishing.com

Bias-free STRESS Measurement

A practical approach to understanding the human response to stresses that is explained from the materials sciences viewpoint through the use of common, every day examples with which we are all familiar.

The book recognizes that we are all capable of experiencing stresses without, necessarily, experiencing distress or illness. It discusses the human ability to respond to stresses as a result of internal strength (fortitutde) that is termed Stress Readjustment Energy (SRE), and it provides a measurement scale for pro-active recognition and determination of the levels of individual abilities to deal with stresses.

Calvin K. Preddie, B.Sc., Ph. D.

A bias-free stress measurement rating system

A practical guide for understanding and managing an individual's responses to various life stresses.

A proactive approach to stress management

Definition of Stress

"*Stress is produced by any thing, or experience that requires a measure of adjustment by the human system in order to maintain the normal or natural balanced state of the total body system to which an individual has become accustomed.* This includes the physical, mental, emotional, intellectual, financial and other lifestyle states in which the individual exists. Anything that might disturb any aspect of the internal and environmental balanced state of an individual in a positive or negative way produces stress." (page 41)

"Except in the case of sickness, life stresses do not represent any form of illness. They are a normal and necessary part of our existence. But when stresses become so severe that an individual is unable to deal wth them without suffering some detrimental effect(s), it is possible that they could lead to illness. Fortunately, the human system appears to have been provided with an amount of natural **Stress Readjustment Energy (SRE)** to enable us to deal with many individual and combined stress experiences successfully. We are also provided with reserve SRE to help us cope beyond our normal limits, when stress experiences persist to take us beyond our **Stress Readjustment Energy Limit (SREL)**, which is similar to the "Proportional Limit" for inanimate material." (page 42)

"Any type of stress, and the struggle to overcome it, as well as the inability to overcome it could lead to other stress complications in unrelated areas. The reports of "air rage" and "road rage", while they may be, correctly, related to stress problems, may not have anything to do with travel pressures. These types of situations, in many cases, could be caes similar to that of "misplaced agression." (page 50)

"We must also remember that the partners are people who would be experiencing other stresses at the same time that marital stress affects their lives. Workplace, social, health, financial and other stress-producers are also being experienced and force the utilization of stress re-adjustment energy that could be partly resposible for any weakness that might encourage the seeking of love re-assuring experiences outside their marriage." (Page 57)

A Notable case of human stress failure resulting in death

The date is August 11, 2000. I have just completed a re-write of my manuscript, Understanding Human Reaction to *Stress*, and I am awaiting the arrival of my *Stress* Reaction Charts from Mail Boxes Inc., who were preparing overheads for me. The morning news tells us about a woman who jumped in front of a moving subway train in Toronto, Ontario, Canada, while clutching her 6-momth old baby in her arms. *Some unfortunate person, who was overcome by the stresses in her life*, I thought. I was not wrong, but as the story was told in the **Toronto Star** newspaper of August 12, 2000, I was completely surprised. This was not any ordinary "Jane Doe"! She was a successful physician and psychotherapist, who counseled patients who were experiencing depression. She was a person who enjoyed the trappings of success, and who had parked her 1999 Mercedes Sports Utility vehicle in a nearby parking lot and walked to the subway station at the start of the rush hour around 6:30 a.m. But more surprising was the news that the night before (August 10, 2000) she was intercepted by police on two occasions (at 10:30 p.m. and 1:30 a.m.), when she was standing close to the tracks with her baby in her arms. It appears that in both instances police officers had been alerted to her suspicious actions. It was not clear, who had contacted the police, but after the second occurrence, police accompanied her back to her home and alerted her family.

Later stories in the press indicated that she was depressed and was under a 24 hour watch, prior to placing her in a psychiatric institution, which was supposed to occur the morning she took the drastic measure to attempt to kill herself and her child. She succeeded to kill the child instantly, but she lived on for several days before succumbing to her injuries.

This lady was obviously *stressed* above the limits of her capacity to deal with the *stresses* in her life. She would have been at the highest level shown on the bias-free *stress* measurement scale discussed in this book. Utilization of my scale and acceptance of the definition of stress given in this work could have, proactively, alerted the lady to the extent of her situation, and might have assisted her to accept the need for outside assistance. It is possible, that her reaction to the idea of being placed in a psychiatric institution to be treated for depression (the same type of ailment that she had helped so many people to overcome) was the final *stress* burden that she could not bear. The combination of *stresses* probably caused her to be taken beyond her stress re-adjustment limit (**SREL**) and could have caused her to attempt drastic action of avoidance for herself and her child. *Stress* Re-adjustment Energy Limit (SREL) is discussed in this work.

The following pages contain examples of human response to stress (stressors), as taken from the pages of the Toronto Star Newspaper in Ontario, Canada.

This letter was published in the HAVE YOUR SAY column of the **Toronto Star** of Sunday October 21, 1990, page D. 3, under the headline, "**She retired early to avoid the TTC at rush hour:**

> "We have been reading a lot about the deplorable service on the subway and TTC, so much that I feel compelled to write and add my voice to the complaints. I believe that what we are reading is just the tip of the iceberg.
>
> Conditions on the Yonge line and particularly, Bloor station, where I get on and off, have become so bad that I have had to give notice in to my job. I simply cannot face another winter riding on the cattle cars and putting up with the push-shove situation that it has become.
>
> I have been travelling daily for the past eight years by bus and subway to the Bloor and Bay area, but the past two and three years have become simply intolerable. At times there is hardly room to stand in the cars, let alone get a seat. We are repeatedly bumped off trains and almost always the platform at Bloor and Yonge is 6-10 people deep.
>
> We have been subjected to all the elements waiting in the old outdoor parking area at York Mills to get to our buses for over three years now. There are no explanations for the delays and grouchy drivers who seem to hate their lot in life.
>
> Although I have less than two years to go to full retirement and enjoy my job tremendously, I feel that my general health and well being is a priority. The TTC is not the better way and I am counting the days till I won't have to suffer the mental and physical abuse of our public transportation system."

The letter was signed, Shirley Allen, Willowdale

This letter is an excellent example of a human response to a *stress*-producing event. This lady's *stress* would probably have manifested itself in the workplace, where it would have been considered workplace stress. It is an example of an individual who, probably, understood the cause of her discomfort, and who acted prior to allowing the *stress* to take her to a possible *distress* level. It represents the kind of pro-active response that the bias-free *stress* measurement (based on the materials sciences approach to stress, would encourage.

This **Toronto Star** story was published July 06, 1999, page A-2, headlined: **Unwanted promotion depresses clerk**

> "BIRMINGHAM (Reuters) – A British office worker was awarded some $150,000 in compensation for job-related stress yesterday because she became depressed after being promoted against her will.
>
> Former Birmingham City Clerical worker Beverley Lancaster, 44, retired on health grounds after being appointed to a more senior post, a court heard.
>
> She said the city council broke promises to offer her training and support for the senior job, for which she had absolutely no experience or qualifications.
>
> After being promoted in 1993, she was repeatedly off sick before she retired in 1997. Judge Frances Kirkham said she agreed that Lancaster's job had apparently resulted in psychiatric illness.
>
> After the hearing, Lancaster said: 'I should still be working. My employers should have listened to me but I was treated like a number, not a human being'."

This is a most interesting story, because most people might consider a promotion on the job to produce positive *stress.* It is also interesting because it sets a precedent that should be a warning to employers about hiring employees who are not properly prepared and supported for the carrying out of assigned duties. It is, probably, also a precedent that could be used by employees and other staff to charge employers for being responsible for *stressful* situations that could be considered to result from being placed in inappropriate job positions. People who are forced to work for welfare and suffer *stress* disorders as a result, may also be able to sue; as would teachers who are forced to give their private time for after school programs, some of which they are not qualified to supervise.

This story highlights the type of *stress* experience that could result from asking an engineer to accept a management position, or a manager to perform technical functions during a labor dispute. There might also be situations where employers could be held financially responsible for *stress* caused to other members of a family because of situations where forced job responsibilities cause problems. This would be the case, where there is lack of supervision of a young child because the parent (a teacher) is forced to supervise an after school program.

This third story was published in the **Toronto Star** dated February 22, 2000, page A-16. It was written by Workplace Issues reporter, Vanessa Lu. It was titled: **Former guard to be compensated for stress** and it is presented below.

> "A former Kingston prison guard suffering from chronic stress will receive compensation after the Workplace Safety and Insurance board reversed an earlier decision. 'It's a tremendous victory for this particular worker,' said her lawyer, David Wilken.
>
> The 52-year old woman, whose name has been withheld, could receive more than $100,000 in compensation retroactive to 1995, when she stopped working. She could also be eligible for future annual compensation of up to 90 per cent of her net earnings.
>
> In December, the Workplace Safety and Insurance Appeals Tribunal ruled the woman qualified for compensation for chronic mental stress because of her 15 years as a correctional officer. The Tribunal said it has 'no doubt that the worker's workplace was a psychologically hostile environment'.
>
> The woman is so traumatized she won't leave her seventh-floor apartment, which has bars on the windows, because she might encounter former inmates or co-workers.
>
> She said she suffered harassment and verbal abuse from male guards from 1980 until 1995.
>
> The tribunal ruled the woman was eligible for compensation, but it was unclear whether the previous board's policy against compensating for chronic stress applied in her case. The board decided last Friday it's previous policy 'had not been established through a formal enough process to be considered a policy.' The board expects to issue a statement on what constitutes policy in the future.
>
> This woman's case will not open the floodgates for compensation because only 30 similar cases are pending, said Laurie Hardwick of the Ontario Federation of Labour."

This is a case of workplace stress that could possible be considered a precedent for determining whether a job related situation contributes to *stress* that affects individuals to the point of rendering them incapable of providing useful service.

This fourth story, which is not being presented in its entirety, was published in the **Toronto Star**, dated April 07, 1993, page B. 1. It was written by, Alison Cunliffe, and it carried the headline, **Hardships of night jobs take stiff toll, experts say**.

> "The hardships of night work are so tough that 20 per cent of shift workers can't take it and quit," a health and safety consultant says.
>
> And the impact of shift work is growing, Elizabeth Dobbin, a consultant with the Ontario Pulp and Paper Makers Safety Association said yesterday. While 27 per cent of Ontario employees already work shift, the number will grow to one out of three before the trend to shift work peaks", she said.
>
> "If people work when their bodies want to sleep, the result is unhappy employees with health problems, absenteeism and low morale," said Dobbin, who specializes in helping to reduce problems with shift work.

The story continues by discussing the problems for shift workers, and the hidden costs for employers such as, bigger overtime bills and expensive accidents. It ends with a general statement that: "Night workers can help themselves by eating better, staying fit and experimenting with bright lights in the early evening just before work." This type of generalized solution for every shift worker does not consider the different needs of individuals. It does not recognize that some individuals might enjoy shift work for many different reasons, and may not be as *stressed* out as others, who have legitimate reasons for being affected by shift duties.

This story should alert employers to their responsibility for the work environment, which could contribute to increased *stress* in employees and staff. A proactive approach to human reaction to *stress* might be able to alert individuals and employers to potential problems before they are allowed to happen.

Introduction to the bias-free stress measurement scale

The need for a bias-free stress measurement scale is covered in a later chapter, but a brief introduction to the scale might be helpful.

In the material sciences, every material is different and possesses different individualistic properties for resisting different types and levels, as well as several combinations of stress. However in analyzing stress in materials, we embrace the "Principle of Elasticity" from which we know that every material responds to imposed stress in a proportional manner up to a limiting value (The Proportional Limit) by utilizing an appropriate amount of resistance to carry, or support the imposed stress.

By applying a similar type of analysis based on the recognition that each individual is different (DNA, fingerprints, eyes, voice, teeth, footprint and other physical and intellectual facets), and that each of us have the ability to deal with some level of stress without noticeable negative effects, the Author has developed a technique for each individual to pro-actively determine his, or her reaction to life stresses. Many common, everyday situations are utilized to explain the individual nature of human reaction to stress.

The system should permit individuals to obtain early warning that a stress situation is becoming unbearable and might require assistance beyond what the individual is capable of providing to prevent the stress situation from becoming one of distress. Since it is the individual's perception that becomes the reality, the person's reaction to a scale that deals with the person's perception is expected to produce results at least as meaningful, and perhaps more reliable than the explanations and rationalizations that might be conveyed to a therapist of counselor.

The Author suggests that in many situations, individuals do not address the stress or stresses they face until it has become distress, consequently, what we now call stress is, probably, distress. This would mean that stress might have already become an illness by progressing to a state beyond which the individual has the capability to resist because of internal fortitude. The Author considers this point to be beyond the SREL (Stress readjustment energy limit) that is comparable to the Proportional Limit for materials.

Since the Author's stress measurement scale is linked to individual reactions that are expressed in a form to permit individual assessment and interpretation, there should be little or no bias in the results. This method is different than one which uses a scale with an arbitrarily determined value for retirement that does not consider whether the individual who is retiring has planned successfully for the retirement, and/or whether the retirement is by choice or is forced; or by an arbitrarily selected fixed numerical value for stress caused by the Christmas season without any consideration about the religion of the individual.

The Author's system would not be perfect and would require practice to become used to it. However it is based on a belief that an individual cannot tell a lie to his or her self, unless one is in "denial" in which case reliable information is doubtful. Each individual is considered to be in the best position to determine how a stress has affected them. It is this knowledge and an individual's interpretation of the effects of the stress experienced that provides the information for using the bias-free stress measurement scale.

Calvin Preddie

HOW TO HANDLE STRESS

1 *Use your MasterCard to pay your VISA*
2 *Pop some corn without putting on the lid*
3 *When someone says: "Have a nice day," tell them you have other plans*
4 *Make a list of things to do that you have already done*
5 *Forget the diet center and send yourself a candy gram*
6 *Print "OUT TO LUNCH" on your forehead*
7 *Leaf through a National Geographic and draw underwear on the natives*
8 *Dance naked in front of your pets*
9 *Put your youngster's clothes on him backwards and send him to daycare*
10 *Retaliate for tax increases by filing your tax return in Roman Numerals*
11 *Go shopping, buy everything, wear it, and return it all the next day*
12 *Buy a subscription to a sleazy magazine and send it to your boss*
13 *Pay your hydro bills in pennies*
14 *Drive to work in reverse*
15 *Sit naked on a shelled, hard-boiled egg*
16 *Tell your boss to blow it out his mule (let him figure it out)*
17 *Polish your car with ear wax*
18 *Bill your doctor, dentist, optometrist for time spent in the waiting room*
19 *Braid the hair in each nostril and each ear*
20 *Write a short story using alphabet soup or Alpha bits cereal*
21 *Eat celery naked in bed, using your navel to hold the salt to dip the celery in*
22 *Stare at people through the tines of a fork and pretend they are in jail*
23 *Make up a language and ask people for directions*

24 *Make a lunch date with your dog or cat and honor it*

25 *Take moon baths*

IF THE ABOVE FAILS, EAT THIS PAGE AND WASH IT DOWN WITH SODA OR WINE. REMEMBER LAUGHTER IS ONE OF THE BEST STRESS-BUSTERS THERE IS.

These suggestions (source unknown) were found on my desk at the College where I worked, and where I offered a seminar on Human Reactions to Stress for a group of Senior citizens.

Whilst it is all about laughter, we may note that suggestion number one has become a favorite means by which some credit card companies try to relieve financial stress by inviting potential clients to pay off their balance on a competitive credit card by assigning it to their card at a favorable interest rate for a limited time period.

Calvin Preddie

Dedication

During my second semester, as a civil engineering student at university, in 1958, my Social Sciences Professor said to me, "*I don't know if you are as good on the drawing board as you are in this course, however, I think your future is in the social sciences.*" He then proceeded to tell the class a story about a discussion between a doctor, a lawyer and an engineer, about which is the finest profession.

The doctor, he told us, said that God created man, which is the ultimate medical feat, therefore medicine must be the finest profession. Then, the lawyer reminded the doctor about the Ten Commandments, which still represented the apex of legal direction, so he insisted that law must be the finest profession. The engineer then told them, that he (it was several years ago) did not know which was the finest profession. However, he said, in the beginning, God created heaven and earth, and the entire universe that is still unfolding, and he (the engineer) was certain that it was, and always will be, the greatest engineering achievement.

Later, as a teacher of students of civil engineering and mechanical engineering technology, I often reminded them of the important responsibility that was placed upon the engineering team of engineer/technologist/technician/tradesperson. I would begin by pointing out that whether we were guilty of a crime or not, the law demanded that we be represented by a lawyer, and we accepted this without placing any requirement that the lawyer be successful. In cases of illness—even those considered incurable, we would visit a doctor without any pre-condition that we be cured; and we would visit psychiatrists without any guarantee of a successful adjustment after their efforts. However, I would ask them, if you approached a new bridge and inquired of the engineer, whether the bridge would stand up or not; and if he/she replied that sometimes it might, and sometimes it might not, would you drive across? The answer was, usually, no. Perhaps, my Social Sciences Professor, even more than some of us in the field of engineering, was more alert about the impact of engineering and technology in our lives.

This book is dedicated to Professor Martin; to human life, and to the indomitable human spirit.

Calvin K. Preddie, P. Eng.

"It seems to me that a way of life based on the understanding of man's responses to stress and to constant change is the only way that leads out of the present jungle of conflicting judgments about right and wrong, justice and injustice, in which our sense of values have become entangled and obscured."

Dr. Hans Selye
Stress Without Distress, 1975

"Personality is that core of thoughts and feelings inside you that tells you how to conduct yourself. It is a checklist of responses, based on innate values and strongly held beliefs. It directs your emotional as well as your rational reaction to every life experience."

Dr. Taylor Hartman
The Color Code, 1987

"Engineers' concern for the effects of stress has enabled them to devise safety factors to ensure that materials are not over-stressed. Their analyses are governed by the theory of Stress and Strain, with which all engineers are familiar. Engineers have determined for materials, the stress levels that Dr. Selye recommends for human comfort."

Calvin Preddie
An Engineering Analysis of Man's Reaction To Stress, 1974

Author's Note

The ideas, procedures and suggestions contained in this book are **not** intended to be substitutes for consulting with your physician, or mental health specialist. All maters regarding your mental and physical wellness require medical supervision.

Calvin K. Preddie

Table of Contents

Foreword

Human beings experience many and different types of *stress* every day of their lives. In dealing with these *stresses*, it is not a simple case of choosing to manage our lives so that we can experience the "Joy of Stress", as suggested in Dr. Peter Hanson's book, nor is it the pure situation of experiencing (positive) stress without (negative) stress, as suggested in Dr. Selye's book, "Stress without Distress". Dealing with *stress* is more complex than the application of Dr. Hanson's three principles of stress management: (1) "Pamper yourself within your budget"; (2) "Stop stonewalling", and (3) "Face the truth." Dealing with *stress* is not the simple case of making "a success of life by enjoying its challenging stress without suffering distress", as indicated by Dr. Selye. Human beings would be able to deal with *stress* better, and be able to guard against excesses of *stress,* if we could become aware of our abilities to react to different types and levels of *stress.* However, to do so, it would be necessary for us, at the physical, mental and emotional levels, to be able to develop a better understanding of the relationship between our responses to *stress,* and the *stresses* we must experience each day, as part of our existence.

Consider a family with two spouses, who are both employed, and who have recently purchased a home for their two teen-aged children and themselves, because they considered themselves to be secure in their employment with their employers. Without any advance notice, the male partner's employers decide that cut backs are needed to improve the bottom line, and he is served notice that his job would cease to exist in two month's time. At age 45, he knows that the job market does not hold many prospects at the time, and his spouse and himself had endured endless sacrifices to purchase their home, for which they would be unable to continue the payments after the small settlement amount he receives is used up. Both he, and his spouse, would experience severe financial *stress,* until their situation improves. The children, too, would probably feel the effects of the situation, especially, if it impacts negatively on their ability to make purchases and to join friends on outings and in extra curricular activities. Would pampering themselves (within the family's budget), or facing the truth remove the financial *stress* to bring joy into the family's existence? Is there any way the family could make a success of life by enjoying the heavy financial burden, without experiencing distress? How would decompressing, or triggering a relaxation response aid the family in dealing with the *stress?*

There are many actions the family could take to reduce, or even to escape, the financial *stress* burden, but there is also the risk that one, or all, of the choices could cause the family to experience different types of *stress* for which they may be unprepared. The new *stress*, while reducing the financial *stress*, could produce personal relationship *stresses* that could result in the breakup of the family, and could, actually, produce other *stresses,* including other new forms of financial *stress.*

The same type of analysis would be appropriate, if we were considering the reaction of a family forced to deal with a parent suffering from Alzheimer's disease, or from incurable cancer, or from AIDS.

We will not, always, be able to manage our lives in a manner that would help us to avoid onerous *stresses*, nor may we be able to avoid distress from *stress*-producing situations. However, if we have a clearer understanding of the types and levels of *stress* that we are capable of enduring, there is a better chance for us to lessen the occurrence of distress levels. We would be armed with the ability to seek out experiences to make our lives more joyful, and more successful, despite the distress and sadness of the negative stressful events we may be forced to experience.

Background

My interest in applying the engineering theory of stress in materials to the analysis of *stress* in humans was sparked in the second summer during my studies at Howard University, Washington, DC USA. The previous summer, my brother and I had perpetrated a small deception by stating that I was a pre-med student. That statement, and the fact that he (a pre-med student at the time) had been an employee at the Overlook Hospital in Summit, New Jersey, USA, led to my employment as an Orderly at the hospital. Because it was believed that I was studying to become a doctor, during my second summer of employment, I was assigned duties in the operating room.

I had recently completed a course of study in Strength of Materials, as part of my civil engineering studies. In that course, we discussed the fact that, relatively speaking, a single strand of human hair was stronger, in resisting a tensile (pulling) force than a strand of steel of similar size (diameter). One day, as I observed hammers and chisels being used in the repair of broken bones on elderly patients, I became, instantly, fascinated with the comparison of the human skeletal structure to the skeletal framing structure of a building. I was intrigued by the fact that a human could experience such damage to a main structural member, have it repaired, and have it regain full use after a short recuperative period. I knew that should the main member of the framework of a building be ruptured, the entire structure would probably collapse, and would require demolition and a complete rebuilding over several months, before it could be reused. It is from my musings that summer, that many comparisons between human beings and engineering materials was spawned.

I began to wonder whether man would ever design a man-made pump to function as unceasingly, and as precisely, as the human heart. I tried to think of a computer with the simultaneous processing capability, and the storage capacity, of the human brain. To me, the water supply and waste disposal systems, so important to the functions of the daily life of humans, paled in comparison with the blood supply and waste disposal systems in the human body. The human electronic system of nerves and sensors seemed much more sophisticated than anything man could design; and the structural design and function of the human skeletal frame far surpassed anything man could, or would ever produce. For some unexplained (probably serendipitous) reason, my thoughts focused in on the comparison of human *stress* and stress in materials.

These thoughts led to my article, "Could the engineering theory of stress and strain be applied to life", which was published in the Howard Engineer magazine in 1961. After the publication of the article, I was confronted by a problem that prevented me from exploring the matter further at that time—it was the difficulty of measuring *stress* in humans. At the time, I speculated that hypnotism, or hallucinogenic drugs would have to be utilized to create illusions of actual *stress* to obtain useful measurements—if it were even possible to obtain such measurements. My thoughts remained with me, and they, first, resurfaced significantly 11 years later.

In 1972, I read in a Montreal, Quebec, Canada newspaper that human *stress* researchers had found that when a *stress* was removed from the body, stability returns, but if the *stress* was prolonged, the body's defense system gradually wore down and deterioration followed. This finding mirrored the behavior of materials up to, and beyond the Proportional Limits of the materials. The newspaper article prompted me to rewrite the article with a more positive title, "An Engineering Analysis of Man's Reaction to Stress". I entered the piece in a Writer's Digest competition, where it was a awarded a 43rd prize. Emboldened by the small success, I sent copies of my article to Dr. Hans Selye, at the Université de Montreal, and to stress researchers at the Harold Brunn Institute in California, USA.

The late, Dr. Hans Selye, who, during his life, was considered the foremost authority on human *stress*, responded May 29, 1972, to say that he had read the article, "*with interest and profit.*" He also commented on a "typo" which, I believe, occurred when I addressed the envelope to Hans "Seyle" instead of Hans Selye. In May of the same year, Dr. Ray H. Rosenman, M.D., Assistant Director of the Harold Brunn Institute at Mount Zion Hospital and Medical Centre, in California, USA, also replied. He stated that he found the *"analogy to stress and strain in building materials to be a particularly fascinating one."* He urged that it be submitted to a publication such as the Journal of Psychosomatic Research where, he claimed, *"It would certainly be instructive to all readers."* He added that, "*It would also help us in the conception of our work here.*"

Dr. Selye had asked me to send him a copy of the article, again, after it was published. I sent the article, and a query, to the Journal of Psychosomatic Research, (at the time it was being published in England), and they suggested that I obtain back copies of their Journal and put the article in their customary format. Perhaps I erred in not following through, so that the article would have reached a wider scientific community. However, I chose instead, to have the article published by the Association of Professional Engineers of the Province of Ontario, Canada (APEO). This way I could have it validated by the engineering community to satisfy Dr. Selye's valid need.

After the article was published, I forwarded a copy to Dr. Selye. He responded that he would give the article *"adequate attention"* in a *"Stress Index"* that he was working on, that would summarize *"key publications on stress as applied to various disciplines"*. He requested that I keep him up to date on anything that I published along those lines. I do not know if Dr. Selye completed the Index before his death. Copies of his letters, and the letter from Dr. Rosenman are appended to this book.

I never abandoned the idea about applying the engineering theory of stress in materials to *stress* in human life. My energies were diverted towards the cause of peace and nuclear disarmament, and their relationship to the protection of our environment. I devoted several years to a very satisfactory letter writing exercise of addressing world leaders in an effort, which, to me, has been rewarded by the way in which disarmament and relations between the super powers have proceeded, and are being resolved. The lingering ideas about the analogy between *stress* in humans, and stress in inanimate objects peaked again in the late 1980's after reading Dr. Selye's book, "Stress without Distress, and Dr. Hanson's book, "The Joy of Stress". I wrote the book, with the title, Understanding Human Reaction to Stress, and I sent it out to a few publishers on speculation. My first try was with American Psychiatric Press Inc., Washington, DC, USA, who kept the manuscript for about eight weeks, before I received a letter with the signature of the Editor in Chief. I was advised that they, "have the resources to accept only a limited number of the many proposals and manuscripts submitted" each year, and they wished me "luck" in finding another publisher. Next, a Canadian Publishing House found the book to be, "too theoretical and dedicated to an analysis of the work of Dr. Hanson and Dr, Seyle". They expressed the thought that there was, "insufficient practical advice of the sort that will appeal to the general trade reader". It was signed by the Managing Editor, PTR Division. The Acquisitions Editor replied for the third Press, in the US. The Editor apologized for having, "taken such a long time responding to your interesting proposal." The letter continued, "UNDERSTANDING HUMAN REACTION TO STRESS contains some truly original ideas, as you must know. Unfortunately, we only publish eight books a year...and these must fall into our very particular self-help format." I was thanked for thinking about them, and they enclosed a copy of their catalogue.

A chance meeting with Dr. Taylor Hartman, during a sabbatical with the Ministry of Colleges and Universities, Toronto, Ontario, Canada in 1990, introduced me to Dr. Hartman's ideas about human actions being directed by "motives", "needs", and "wants." His ideas provided me with the answer I needed to establish that differences between individuals was a reality.

I used the time in between this version of the book and the initial manuscript, to investigate a connection between the differences that I believe to exist between individuals, and their "motive", "needs", and "wants." This was in accordance with the concept discussed in Dr. Taylor Hartman's book, "The Color Code", which suggests that through some lottery, at birth, we all fall into one of four Color Codes. These Codes are seen to determine our motives, needs and wants. I have concluded that individual reaction to *stress* is linked to the way that the *stress*-producing event impacts on our individual motives, needs and wants. I am convinced that such a connection exists, but I do not have the permission to include my work in this area in this book because I did not receive permission to include Dr. Hartman's Personality Profile Test as an Appendix in this book. However, I have taken the comments of the previous editors, who were contacted, into consideration. Most of the material that might be considered "technical" now appears in the appendices, and there is a distinct move towards a self-help book as it discusses the use of a bias-free stress rating scale and procedures for its use by individuals. The examination of the works of Dr. Selye, and Dr. Hanson, still exists, but it is treated as background information, and used as justification for my perspective on *stress* reactions in humans, when viewed from a materials sciences standpoint.

After devoting several years to the issue of Canadian unity, I am again motivated to complete this book. I have been driven, partly by some of the new methods being suggested for curing *stress* (including a recent suggestion about utilizing games such as "blowing up the office", and "the beastly boss", as *stress*-busters. I am also partly motivated by a recent legal ruling in the UK, where a woman was compensated as a result of the effects of *stress,* produced by a promotion for which she did not receive any training. I am also motivated by my entry into the business world, as a human resources service provider. I am listed on the Internet, as a non-medical consultant, for assisting people in the use of my bias-free, individualized stress-rating scale that is patterned after the materials sciences approach for inanimate materials, and to encourage individuals to adopt a pro-active approach to dealing with *stress* in our lives.

It has taken a long time, but it is a book that I have to write. It is about something that I have to, and need to share with the world.

Introduction

For human beings, understanding our reactions and performance capabilities while experiencing a particular type, and combinations of, *stress* is more valuable than knowing about the common symptoms of *stress*. These symptoms are reflected in internal chemical and biological changes that could only be measured in research, and medical, facilities. These measurements cannot be made on a regular basis. However, whether we choose to ignore it, or deny it, we are, usually aware that our physical, emotional and mental abilities are affected during periods of *stress*—especially excessive *stress*. We would benefit from a method to identify the types and levels of *stress* that we could comfortably experience, as well as those that we cannot manage, successfully, on our own.

Thanks to the work of other researchers, and the late, Dr. Hans Selye, we know that the common chemical and biological changes that take place in the human body at times of *stress* produce a syndrome that is indicative of the presence of a level of *stress* in our system. It is, probably, the fact that this syndrome can be identified when a level of *stress* is being experienced, that led Dr. Selye, and others to consider *stress* in a manner that causes it to be regarded as a single disease. However, just as the common symptoms of cancer are not the cancer itself, the common symptoms of *stress* do not identify the nature of the *stress* being experienced.

Response Indicator of Human *Stress* Condition

Chemical and biological change experienced by the human body is an excellent and accurate indicator that a *stress* condition is being experienced. However, unless the extent of its presence can be linked to the level of *stress* being experienced, it does not tell us about an individual's ability to resist different types and levels of *stress*. It is the ability to discern the levels and types of *stress* we experience that would provide us with early warning signals that could trigger pro-active responses to prevent us from being exposed to levels of *stress* that could be damaging. Early warning signals would act as indicators that would enable us to attempt timely lifestyle changes, and to seek external assistance to protect us from experiencing onerous stressful situations that could permanently affect our lives.

Effect of Multiple *Stresses*

The symptoms of *stress* do not tell us whether it is produced by a single event, or several events being experienced at the same time. However, every day of our lives, we experience a multitude of *stress*-producing events, some positive, and some negative. Every *stress*-producing experience, whether "positive", or "negative", has an unbalancing effect on the human system. The imbalance is sometimes minor and routine so that we are hardly aware of its existence. Walking, talking, singing and breathing, require effort and energy. Under normal circumstances, these activities do not appear to tax our abilities. However, if we are experiencing *stress* caused by illness, being tired, fear, or by some other circumstance(s), even the simple acts mentioned above tax our energies and become major *stress*-producing sources. There are, however, other events that have immediate effect and produce serious *stress* that, by themselves, and in combination with other events, can cause our *stress* levels to rise to extreme heights. Death of a companion or family member, loss of a job, awaiting an interview and even the winning of a contest sometimes exhaust our abilities to withstand the effect of a single *stress or stresses)* in our lives, and impair our ability to re-establish a balanced state in our bodily systems.

At any time that an individual might be coping with reaction to a combination of *stresses*, it might be possible to put off the need to deal with a particularly disturbing *stress*-producing event. We could, possibly, establish this by changing our environment, or by concentrating on something else in order to put the disturbing event, temporarily out of our thoughts. Such a process (if it could be successfully accomplished) would result in a reduction of the need to utilize energy necessary to re-establish the balanced state of an individual's body. In such a situation, the individual's ability to deal with the remaining *stress*-producing events would be enhanced. Thus, researchers and human *stress* experts are correct in citing wellness and life-style management as keys to avoiding *stress*, when *stress* is considered to require a re-adaptation effort, in response to the unbalanced body system caused by *stress*-producing events.

We should realize, however, that the effort to achieve wellness and lifestyle management also produce *stress*. Therefore, unless individuals are pre-disposed to the disciplined existence required for controlled lifestyles, there could be additional *stresses* caused by the changed life style that could lead to a critical situation, and which could require a significant use of re-adaptation energy.

Dr. Selye's Viewpoint

Dr. Selye, relates what he calls "stress" (which is what the materials sciences call "strain") to the "General Adaptation Syndrome" (GAS). He considers the GAS to be the internal chemical and biological changes that occur as the human body attempts to re-establish internal balance (homeostasis) that is being disturbed as a result of a "stressor" (which is what materials sciences call stress). The fact that similar biological and chemical changes occur under observed "stressor" conditions does appear to justify the interpretation of this syndrome to be indicative of *stress*. Presence of the GAS might suggest the consideration of *stress* as a single disease. However, since we would, probably, all agree that life is stressful, and that we are continually experiencing stress, then the GAS should always be present in our lives. But, if the GAS signals the existence of a level of *stress* that causes us to exhaust our capabilities to re-establish homeostasis, it, quite possibly, signals that we have reached an over-*stress* situation. This situation could be produced by a single event, the extent of a single event, or by a combination of events that disturb the body's balanced system.

The work of Dr. Selye, and other researchers has helped us to understand that "stressors" (*stress)* demand a readjustment effort from the human system, in an attempt to maintain homeostasis (internal balance). But, at a practical level, it would be more helpful to individuals, if there were means to identify the type and levels of *stress*-producing events that might tax the person to a level beyond all available internal re-adaptation resources of which the individual is capable. Medical science and the science of technology and engineering are being utilized in combination for the benefit of humanity in many spheres of life. Similar benefits would, likely, be produced by utilizing engineering knowledge of stress in inanimate materials, in combination with biological and chemical knowledge of human reaction to "stressors" (*stress.)* The combined effort would produce better awareness of human abilities to experience, and to successfully withstand the *stresses* of life.

The Aim of This Book

This book is an attempt to integrate the work of Dr. Selye, and other human *stress* researchers with the engineering approach to stress in inanimate materials, to produce a better understanding of human reaction to *stress*. The book also integrates Dr. Taylor Hartman's concept of personality types that determine our motives and needs, to explain the different reactions of individuals to similar types of *stresses*.

Finally, the book introduces a bias-free *stress* measurement scale and discusses ways in which it could be utilized as a pro-active tool to assist individuals from allowing *stress* experiences to become critical or chronic, to the point of impairing their ability to deal with their personal lives.

Material in this book that could be considered technical will appear in the appendices, where those who might be interested in the material could use it. The rest of the book is written in a manner to allow it to be read, easily, by all, regardless of interest, or ability in the technical aspects of the materials sciences approach to stress in inanimate material.

Comparisons between Terms

Dr. Selye	Materials Sciences	Author
Stress	Strain	Stress Readjustment Energy
Stressor, or Stressor Agent tion	Stress	Stressor, Stress-producing ac- or event, and stress
Adaptation Energy	No term	Reserve Readjustment Energy
Normal Level of Resistance	Proportional Limit	Natural Readjustment Energy Limit
No term	Elastic Region	Natural Readjustment Energy Region
G.A.S. (author's interpretation)	Plastic region	Reserve Readjustment Energy Region
No term	Ultimate Stress	Ultimate Stress Limit
Failure (death)	Rupture/Failure	Failure

An elastic band could explain the materials sciences Principle of Elasticity

The Principle of Elasticity recognizes that when external loads are applied to a material, it experiences internal stress, which triggers an internal strain response that is proportional to the applied stress, up to a critical point called the "Proportional Limit." If loads continue to be applied beyond this critical point, very minor increases produce greater and disproportionate increases in strain reaction, and continued increases would lead to Rupture, or failure. However, below the "Proportional Limit", when the external load is removed, the material would revert to its original ability to resist external stress. We could visualize the Principle of Elasticity by considering the behavior of an elastic band that is being pulled at both ends. Once the pulling forces are removed, the elastic band reverts to its original shape and size. However, if we continue to apply pulling forces, the elastic band reaches a point, where it becomes limp and loses its elastic quality. It would have passed its proportional limit, and continued application of pulling forces would result in its "failure", as it would break apart.

Stress is not a singular illness

People often speak of *stress* in a manner that suggests a single, identifiable condition. Different types of activities are usually advertised as methods for reducing and eliminating *stress* from our lives. Many researchers and counselors also speak of human *stress*, as though it is a single condition of human illness. But *stress* itself is not an illness, even though it could produce illness, and could, possibly cause death.

Definition of *Stress*

***Stress* is produced by any thing, or experience that requires a measure of adjustment by the human system, in order to maintain the normal or natural balanced state of the total body system, to which an individual has become accustomed.** This includes the physical, mental, emotional, intellectual, financial, and other lifestyle states in which the individual exists. Anything that might disturb any aspect of the internal and environmental balanced state of an individual in a positive or negative way produces *stress.* Things such as: illness; debt; joy; sadness; luck; writing exams; physical exertion, and coping with traffic produce *stress* in our lives. So too, do experiences such as: life in a crowd; life in a multicultural society; life in a world in conflict; viewing television news; attending movies, and reading newspapers. Other common and everyday experiences that contribute to *stress* in our lives are normal occurrences. These include things such as: coping with relatives and friends; coping with superiors and subordinates; meeting deadlines; awakening to an alarm clock; commuting on a crowded subway or bus; fears; existing in a world threatened with environmental and nuclear destruction, and a myriad of other events and experiences. In short, life is *stressful.* But every *stress* experience would not cause human illness, nor would it normally impair our abilities to function normally, and would not cause death.

Stresses are a normal part of human existence

Except in the case of sickness, life *stresses*, do not represent any form of illness. They are a normal and necessary part of our existence. But, when *stresses* become so severe that an individual is unable to deal with them without suffering some detrimental effect(s), it is possible that they could lead to illness. Fortunately, the human system appears to have been provided with an amount of natural **Stress Readjustment Energy** (**SRE**) to enable us to deal with many individual and combined *stress* experiences successfully. We are, also, provided with reserve SRE to help us to cope beyond our normal limits, when *stress* experiences persist to take us beyond our **Stress Readjustment Energy Limit** (**SREL**), which is similar to the Proportional Limit for inanimate material.

Evidence that humans, like materials, possess a natural, internal ability to resist imposed *stress* is first demonstrated when an infant is born. Instantly, the newborn is forced to experience life without the assistance of the mother, and it is only in rare instances, when there are mitigating circumstances, that an infant would die from being born. The infant is required to breathe for itself and its body has to deal with an entirely new and unfamiliar environment, which would impose certain *stresses* that are safely handled by the newborn, in most instances. I believe the newborn would experience a *stress* condition that is more critical than for a trained astronaut who is required to walk in space for the first time, even after a prolonged training period on earth.

The existence of natural and reserve readjustment energy could be visualized, if we consider the natural task of walking. A short walk at a normal pace, over the distance of an average city block, requires an output of energy that has a minimal effect on the body of a healthy person. However, if the individual were to walk for a long distance, or for a long period of time, or at a rapid pace, the effect that walking has on the body becomes apparent. The individual becomes, progressively, aware of the energy demands on the body that is reflected in the breathing rate, as additional energy reserves are mobilized to continue the walking exercise. It is not the effort to walk that produces awareness of a *stress* experience, it is the amount, or the pace of walking that causes the individual to feel the effects of the physical *stress* of walking, which could produce the minor health condition of shortness of breath.

Excessive *stress* can produce illness

Excessive, or prolonged, *stress* can produce illness. Illness, however, produces *stress* in the human body, so that whenever illness occurs there would always be the effect of "attending" *stresses* with which an individual must cope. During a period of illness much of the readjustment energy effect experienced is, probably, the result of a combination of the actual need of the body to resist the illness, and the need to direct readjustment energy away from activity required for resisting other *stress* experiences. I believe this would occur, in order to accommodate the more immediate requirement of establishing health balance in the human system.

Despite the fact that individual *stress* producing influences or combinations of *stresses* result in human illness, it would be incorrect to refer to all *stress* as an activity or experience that causes illness. It is only when the *stress* or combination of *stresses,* being experienced demand readjustment energy that the individual is incapable of providing that illness might result. If *stress* persists, and illness is intense or prolonged, it is possible that the individual could be taken to the Stress Re-adjustment Energy Limit, where long-term or permanent incapacitation might result, or even death. A continuation of the *stress* could result in death.

Dr. Selye recognized the problem of identifying stress

Dr. Hans Selye, was very conscious of the difficulties in identifying *stress* as a single illness. In the book, Stress Without Distress, he wrote, "*The word 'stress' like 'success', 'failure', or 'happiness', means different things to different people, so that identifying it is extremely difficult although it has become part of our daily vocabulary.*" He indicated that a variety of conditions produce *stress*, but "*...none of them can be singled out as being it, since the word applies equally to all others.*" Dr. Selye , pointed out, however, that *'medical research has shown that in many respects the body responds in a stereotyped manner, with identical biochemical changes, essentially meant to cope with any type of increased demand upon the human machinery.*" I believe that these statements of Dr. Selye, agree with my contention that many experiences produce different types and levels of *stress*. His statement that the body responds in a stereotyped manner, with identical biochemical changes to cope with any type of increased demand upon the human machinery, also supports my contention that it is the increased demand for *stress* readjustment that results in what we refer to as *stress. Stress,* then, in reality, is an occurrence that results when the human machinery is extended beyond its natural capability to readjust to re-establish homeostasis.

According to Dr. Selye, "*The stress-producing factors* (technically called stressors) *are different yet they elicit essentially the same biological stress response.*" It is clear, that Dr. Selye, considered the human response to be the *stress,* and it explains why he saw the concept of "strain", in engineering, to be analogous to what he considered to be stress. I believe that, his concentration on the stereotyped response led to an analysis of *stress* in a singular context. Every day minor *stress* experiences should not take us to a point where we would have to extend ourselves in any significant manner to restore homeostasis. Therefore, Dr. Selye's words suggest that he was observing an advanced stage of *stress* resistance reaction, which required extra effort from the human system in order to restore homeostasis. I believe that it was excessive, or chronic, *stress* that produced the stereotyped response.

As individuals, we are aware of the stereotyped nature of the production of adrenaline, in response to several human experiences. Fear, joy, success, winning a lottery or losing a fortune, among many other experiences are events that could result in adrenaline stimulation in the human body. However, we are also aware that the need to produce, and the amount of adrenaline produced, would not be the same for each situation. We know, too, that for different individuals, there are different levels of the same type of experience that would be required to stimulate intense adrenaline production. This type of response supports the idea that a particular type, or level, of *stress,* and *stress* combinations would be required for an advanced stage of adrenaline production. This would, more than likely, occur at the distress level.

My ideas do not have major significant differences from the findings of Dr. Selye, and other researchers. If we were to substitute the term *"distress"* for what Dr. Selye calls stress, then it would be logical to assume that the level of activity required to bring an individual to an advanced stage of activity for the re-establishment of homeostasis, would be characterized by the stereotyped response. This would be the stage of excessive *stress.*

The engineering approach should help

By utilizing an approach similar to the one used by engineers to identify stress in inanimate materials, in order to protect against the exposure to excessive stress, we could assist humans to obtain the most joy during our *stressful* existence. We would then be provided with the tool to experience *stress,* successfully, without becoming distressed.

Despite the facility available to engineers to guard against excessive stress in materials, sometimes failures occur for many reasons. In human life, even with a better understanding of our reaction to *stress*-producing experiences, there would be times when failure would occur.

There is no single illness called *stress. Stress* tends to have an effect on the balanced state of the human system, which requires the utilization of readjustment energy to regain a balanced body system. It is the change that materials experience, which permits engineers to identify and predict stress levels for materials; but the change itself, is not the stress. In human life, biological changes that might identify a distress condition that could lead to illness have been identified. We still need to find ways to determine the types and levels of *stress* that we could, safely, experience without being taken to distress levels.

Human *Stress* – A General Analysis

If *stress* were a single illness, there would probably be a single approach to treatment and removal of *stress*. Rather than being a single ailment, there are many events and situations in life that produce *stress* in individuals. Human experience tends to suggest that we are all capable of handling certain amounts of *stress,* however, regardless of the source, or sources, if our total *stress* level were to progress to a state beyond which an individual could handle, successfully, anxiety sets in. It is the onset of anxiety that is the likely trigger of the General Adaptation Syndrome described by Dr. Selye, and which is evidenced in the level of biological and chemical changes that we, commonly, refer to as *stress.* At this point, we are more likely at the distress level, where, if the *stress* is not treated, it could lead to a chronic situation, and possibly, death. When distress occurs, it is more than likely that the individual is reacting, not to a single *stress* experience, but to a combination of a variety, and different levels of *stress* experiences that cause a major unbalanced state that requires major adjustments to return the body to its accustomed state.

***Stress* cannot be removed by removing the symptoms**

If the common *stress* syndrome were actually the *stress*, then it might be possible to remove the *stress* by removing the syndrome, or by counterbalancing the syndrome with induced, opposite, chemical and biological changes. However, as experience would show us, if the source of *stress* was a financial situation, it would not matter what was done about the symptoms, the situation would not go away until it was dealt with through repayment, or forgiveness of the financial obligation.

On the other hand, if an individual's total *stress* situation is the result of several *stress*-producing events, or influences, there might be a way to reduce the total *stress* effect. It would appear logical that, should the individual be able to reduce, or minimize the body's need to respond to one, or a few of the *stress*-

producing influences, then, there would be an increased chance that the individual would be able to withstand the effects of the remaining *stress*-producing influences. A similar situation could, probably, occur, if positive *stress* experiences could be utilized to offset negative ones. The effect of offsetting *stresses* would only last for the duration of the substituted experience (such as a vacation), but it would result in a reduced need to utilize readjustment energy, which could prove helpful once the affecting *stresses* must be accommodated again.

If an individual's lifestyle management is detrimental, such as living beyond one's financial means, or because of an expensive addiction, that contributes, significantly, to the person's total *stress* condition, then it is possible that some action(s) could provide relief. It should be possible to enhance the body's ability to resist the total *stress* condition through improved lifestyle management—provided the changed lifestyle does not create other detrimental *stress* situations. If poor health habits were a significant contributor to a total *stress* situation, improved health care would have a positive effect on an individual's ability to withstand the effects of the remaining *stresses.* The smoking experience should alert us to the possibility of negative effects that a changed lifestyle could produce. For some individuals, giving up the smoking habit could produce other situations (such as weight gain) that could also be *stressful.*

Effects of lifestyle changes

We can make changes in diet, exercise routines, mood-altering experiences like vacations, and utilize other techniques involving meditation and relaxation that could positively affect our well-being and lifestyles. Such changes, while they would permit us to retain unused re-adaptation energy, may not be able to free us, nor protect us from a particular *stress,* or a combination of *stresses.*

The debt *stress* analogy indicates that factors such as, diets, exercise, vacations, relaxation and being honest with yourself cannot remove every *stress*-producing influence from our lives, even though they could produce improved well-being, and a better attitude towards dealing with *stress.*

Other situations, such as the illness *stress* of terminal cancer also indicate how attempts at treatment may be insufficient to alter, or reduce a particular type of *stress.* Treatment and a positive attitude could provide some relief in dealing with the effects of the illness. However, the body stress caused by the cancer cannot be removed. Development of an attitude that permits acceptance of one's situation could help the individual to remain calm, and to avoid hostile feelings that arise from frustration and self-pity, but the cancer situation may not be altered and could become progressively worse. As the body's energy is drained as a result of the disease or treatment, the need to cope with another minor *stress* (such as concern for family) at the same time, could result in a chronic form of *stress* that could lead to complete failure, in the form of death.

Human *stresses* are continuous and constant

There are many sources of *stress* in human life. Human *stress* is also more complex than stress in inanimate materials, because it might be impossible to determine the more dominant influence, which might require the greatest attention for treatment. There is, also, no certain way of calculating relative levels of individual *stresses*, nor levels of combined *stresses* that contribute to the total level of *stress* being experienced at a particular time.

The fact that the human body is constantly resisting *stresses* that are caused by our natural environment, and by personal choices is sometimes forgotten because, like inanimate materials, the human body possesses a natural ability to resist certain *stresses* through *stress* re-adjustment energy (SRE). It is only when the *stress* influences grow in a manner that is out of proportion with our natural abilities to adapt by re-establishing homeostasis that we become acutely aware of our energy consuming efforts to establish a balanced body system. It is likely at this point of awareness that anxiety might begin to occur, and to trigger the General Adaptation Syndrome to which Dr. Selye referred.

While there are some *stresses* that we can, routinely accommodate daily, through our individual readjustment energy levels, there are also some everyday influences for which our normal readjustment energy might be insufficient. Unlike inanimate materials that have a fixed amount of resistance capacity, the human body appears to be blessed with reserve re-adjustment energy that probably exists because of the natural will to survive. Many of these *stresses* are the result of the needs of family life, and the need to work. They include the *stressful* demands of: parenting; coping with married life; handling marriage and a job; dealing with the need to provide the necessities of life for family, and many social needs that arise from our life situations. Even being relieved of the *stresses* produced from parenthood, when children become sufficiently responsible, and being relieved from work pressures because of retirement, produce different types of *stress* influences for individuals.

Workplace *Stress* Considerations

In a world where the work ethic, as it relates to productive work is still held sacred, workplace *stress* begins with the need to have a job. So much is being written about workplace *stress,* currently, that reports appear, almost daily, about the effect of the workplace on the health of individuals, because of work related *stress.* However, workplace *stress* could sometimes be a chicken and egg situation, in determining whether the workplace caused the *stress,* or whether the behaviors attributed to the workplace condition are not a reflection of the effect of *stress* that is brought to the workplace. The individual on the job is the same person who has to deal with financial, marital, health and social obligations that are all capable of causing *stress.* In fact, the time of awakening, and getting to the job cause *stress.* We are also under intense pressure whether we face crowded traffic on the highways, or whether we have to travel on crowded public transportation. Daily *stress,* that could be associated with the requirements of the workplace, do not occur independently of all the other types and levels of *stress* caused by the requirements of life.

At the beginning of this book, I presented some situations dealing with workplace *stress.* One case was a situation, where the individual decided to give up her job to avoid the *stress* of commuting to work by crowded buses and subways. Another case involved an individual, who was promoted against her will and received no training to assist her with being competent in the position. She was awarded compensation for *stress* that resulted from the situation. The third incident involved an individual, who was awarded compensation for mental *stress* because her workplace (where she was a prison guard) was deemed a "*psychologically hostile environment.*" These examples point out the complexity of *stress* reactions in humans, and demonstrate that workplace *stress* is not the simple case of, you go to work, therefore, you are subjected to workplace *stress.*

There are many things to be considered, when we try to analyze workplace *stress.* The type of job, itself, can be the source of severe *stress.* Although the fame and fortune are significant motivating factors, many athletes, choose sports that produce severe physical *stress,* in addition to the *stress* of an uncertain family and social life because of the possibility of being traded, and the need for frequent travel. For some athletes, traveling by plane is *stressful*, and they may choose another form of transportation for the trip. Other individuals choose jobs as policemen and firemen despite the exposure to very *stressful* conditions. Someone who is, or thinks that he, or she, is an intellectual would experience tremendous *stress* if forced to accept a menial job. Such an activity would be one where the most important function might be observation of a warning light so that an appropriate person could be contacted, or a certain process set in motion by the pressing of a button. A successful scientist or engineer could, easily, be placed in an over-*stress* situation if promoted to management; just as a management-oriented person could be unduly *stressed* if required to perform technical functions. These situations suggest that Dr. Hanson and Dr. Selye, are correct when they advise us about choosing the correct job! However, in many instances we may not be aware of which job is correct for us, and economic needs and job availability will often dictate the type of jobs we select, or are forced to accept. Job selection is a definite source of great *stress.*

The importance of understanding the nature of workplace *stress*, and determining whether the job is causing the problem, or whether the problem was brought to the job and was reflected in the attitudes taken on the job could be understood from a couple of newspaper stories in the early 1990's. A May 1991 story in The **Globe and Mail** in Toronto, Ontario, Canada, reported that a Northwestern National Life Insurance Company published results of a study drawn from interviews with a representative sample of 600 US workers. The study was reported to indicate that job *stress* causes frequent health problems for a majority of workers and has led nearly a third of them to seriously consider quitting. The insurance company's records were reported to show that stress-related disability payments cost employers an average of $73,270 per case according to company records from 1982 to 1990. Another May 1991 **Financial Post** report told of a 25 year study by the University of Tulsa that indicated managers had a greater impact on employees than their spouses. We can imagine what the costs per case would be in 2000 and beyond, if a way is not found to determine the causes of *stress* that are visibly reflected in the workplace.

Any type of *stress*, and the struggle to overcome it, as well as the inability to overcome it, could lead to other *stress* complications in unrelated areas. The reports of "air rage" and "road rage", while they may be correctly related to *stress* problems, may not have anything to do with travel pressures. These types of situations, in many cases, could be cases similar to that of "misplaced aggression." Before we identify the condition to be occurring because of the *stress* of driving, or flying, individuals should be carefully questioned about the state of their lives. It could be that other conditions in our society, such as excess taxation, the cost of fuel, too many heavy-handed decisions by our political leaders, and a host of other pressures might cause individuals to experience a sense that all control of their lives has been wrested from them. Maybe, the one thing that gives them the illusion of control is the power to control their cars (very powerful machines). Thus when another individual appears to invade the only space where the individuals feel they have control, they react with negative behavior. In the case of "air rage", it could be a case of a type of "claustrophobic" fear. We must also consider that these individuals, in addition to any *stress* that might be produced by their immediate environments, are also subject to many other *stress* influences that are being carried around with them at the same time. There is no question that work-related *stress*, as would any other type of *stress*, could lead to the development of negative behaviors such as: a drug dependency habit; abuse of alcohol; the abuse of spouses and children, and many other activities that eventually produce excessive *stresses* of their own. What is more significant, and more important, is the fact that we are often unaware of the relationship between any undesirable habit that is developed, and the *stress*-producing source that causes it.

A situation that can be cited to reflect a problem that is being caused by an unrelated event, might surface in the area of marital conflict that stems from a work situation. A person, who is accustomed to making major managerial decisions on the job, daily, would find it very difficult to be subject to reliance on the authority and direction of a spouse, or parent at home. The *stress* that might result from the internal conflict the person experiences could result in a significant and destructive form of marital stress that could result in the break up of the family, and produce severe *stress*, not only for the spouses, but for children, family and friends as well.

Work and other normal life activities can create *stress* in individuals which result in a form of transference of the effects of the *stress*, so that it produces reactions in other activities that are unrelated to the situation that is causing the *stress*. A report published in an August 1991, New England Journal of Medicine supports the idea of "transference". The report dealt with a 1991 study conducted at the Medical Research Council Common Cold Unit in Salisbury, England, where it was found that problems such as: losing a job; breaking off an engagement, or simply feeling overwhelmed by life's burdens, nearly doubles the risk of catching a cold. These results were described as "the first evidence of an association between stress and a biologically verifiable infectious disease." This report was from Boston (AP), and it was published in the **Toronto Star** of August 1991, pg. E 7. These are cases where workplace related *stresses* are transferred to health *stresses*.

Even the possibility that "transference" could be a reality in cases of *stress* reactions, should be enough to warrant a closer inspection of *stress* conditions that are considered to be work related. For employers, it is important because of the high costs that might be involved. For individuals, it would be important they are better able to identify the source(s) of their problems so that the correct types of remedies could be applied, in order to control or improve the situation so that they could enjoy more satisfactory lives. This idea of transference justifies a pro-active approach to understanding our reaction to the many *stresses* we face in life. According to a Conference Board of Canada study of, *Workplace Solutions for the Stressed-Out Worker*, which was reported in the **Toronto Star** of September 08, 1999, pp C 1 and C 5, it was indicated that there is no template for introducing wellness programs into work environments. The same report cited a study by Carleton University in Ottawa, Canada that estimates $2.7 billion to be squandered in lost labor time each year. The report stated, "In today's workplace, where technology spits out reams of e-mail, faxes and voice mail, fuelling desk rage and telephone tempers, and work gets more demanding over-all, employee stress rise." The report talked about asking, "how can we make managers aware of their responsibility to make the place of work more conducive (to productivity) and also to learn to consider employees not as a group, but as individuals with different needs." The individual approach to people's reaction to *stress,* which is reflected in the bias-free *stress* measurement rating scale, would aid the consideration of people as individuals with individual needs.

Some questions that should be considered, and asked when workplace *stress* is suspected

The workplace produces *stress* for all workers (management, staff, and other employees), however, it is important to make an attempt to identify the nature of the *stress* being experienced by someone who complains of experiencing workplace *stress.* A list of some of the questions that should be pursued by the individuals, through self-analysis, and with counselors and friends or family are given below. There is no recommended order for the questions, and responses to some of the questions might trigger other lines of questions, and possibly different questions. The individual should be advised that there are neither right, nor wrong answers to the questions, only honest ones; and should be assured that there is no average set of answers to which the answers given would be compared. The person should be very aware that his/her reaction to *stress* is an individual issue, and would be treated as such.

Is there anything about the job that you enjoy?

Are you able to identify when you began to experience this stress?

What caused you to identify a workplace stress problem?

How do you get (travel) to work?

Do you experience stress from the method used to commute to work?

Do you feel stress in anticipation of being at work, or does it begin when you arrive?

Does the stress become apparent immediately upon arriving on the job, or does it commence at a particular time?

Do you have any close friends among your associates?

In terms of what you would like to achieve personally and professionally, is your job satisfying?

Are you usually satisfied with your job evaluations?

When you feel stressed on the job, how do you react?

Do you react in a similar manner when experiencing other types of stress?

How long have you been on the job in this current position?

Were you stressed out in any previous position?

What is the difference between this job, and any other job you did that did not produce stress?

How is your social, personal and marital life?

Can you think of any other stress-producing situation that exists concurrently with your job stress?

If you could change anything in your job, what would it be?

Do you think that another position in the company would be more satisfying?

How is your relationship with your supervisor, employees and subordinates?

The questions listed above, and several others could assist an individual and an analyst to get a better understanding of the conditions surrounding the individual's current situation, which might show whether there is a definite job problem that is a major contributor to the *stress* situation that is affecting an individual's condition. However, it would serve everyone better, if these questions are asked by individuals of themselves, in a pro-active approach to dealing with personal *stress* problems.

Therapeutic Effect of a change in environment on individual *stress* caused by the workplace

In the book, "Stress without Distress", Dr. Selye tells of the therapeutic value of taking a vacation as a change from *stresses* of the workplace. The changed routine would provide temporary relief from the workplace *stress*, but it does nothing to protect you from it upon your return to work. The change, also, does not tell you anything about your ability to withstand the workplace *stress* without experiencing serious *distress*. The temporary relief occurs as the mind and body concentrate on adaptation to the changed environment and circumstances, and also from enthusiasm for experiencing new places, things and friendships without having to deal with the workplace. However, this would only happen, if your personality would allow you to put the workplace completely out of your mind for the duration of your vacation. If, on the other hand, your personality renders you disposed to take the workplace worries along with you, on your vacation, then the vacation might only add to your *distress*.

As the workplace *stresses* are temporarily forgotten, resistance energy needed for re-establishing balance, as a result of the workplace situation would not be necessary. The need for less re-adaptation energy would be reflected in an enhanced feeling of well-being, which would permit the individual to enjoy the vacation. and the individual's ability to deal with any other *stress*-producing influence would be enhanced. The unused re-adjustment energy would be available for dealing with any new vacation *stresses*.

The same thing would be true, if a vacation were taken to provide relief from *stress* caused by a financial situation. Enjoying the vacation and being able to put the financial situation out of your mind for a short period would provide the similar advantage of unused re-adjustment energy. However, as the financial *stress* would not be reduced as a result of the vacation, and because of the possibility that the financial situation could be worsened, it could lead to increased *stress* levels that could become critical, once the vacation is over.

There is one other consideration that should be examined when we think of workplace *stress*. Sometimes, the workplace could actually provide beneficial relief from *stress*. On one occasion, I discussed, with a friend, the causes of *stress* in her life. Although the person admitted to felling *stressed* because of the distance and the route she drove to get to her job, she indicated that the love of driving her car reduced the *stress* effect of the travel. However, the real surprise was her admission that on arriving at the job, the presence of friends and colleagues would "brighten" her day immediately. Thus, for some, the workplace might provide lifestyle and health improvements, and produce beneficial *stress*. In general, taking a vacation for relieve from *stress*, could be the wrong type of therapeutic experience, if the change might result in more *stress* at the end of the experience.

Understanding the relationship of activity to *stress* levels is important to protect us from exposing ourselves to excess *stress*, unless it is advantageous for to do so. We need to be able to identify the experiences that would cause us *distress*, so that we could try to avoid them. This is the type of thing that engineers do with inanimate materials. They determine the stress limits and capabilities under different types of load situations and then design structures that would not be stressed to critical levels. The *Stress* Rating Scale being proposed in this book is based on the engineering method. There is no way to make the measurement of individual *stress* capabilities a perfect science, but the proposed Stress Rating Scale would be a step forward. It could result in a pro-active effort by each individual to know their reactions to different types and levels of *stress,* which could enhance their selectivity with regard to exposure to *stress.*

Marital *stress*

Marriage is also a very important contributor to severe forms of *stress* in our lives. The falsehood that two people become one, in marriage, has made a significant contribution to the rise of *stressful* situations in the marriage environment. *Stress* research practitioners point to the importance of choosing the right mate as an aid to reduced *stress* in our lives. However, even if one were able to select the "right" mate, at one point in time, there would be other important criteria that must be met. It would require that similar, or complementary, changes occur in both individuals at the same time, and at approximately the same pace for the "oneness" aspect of marriage to continue and to be effective. Since both partners are probably experiencing different work environments, and are subject to the influences of different people and events for a major portion of each day, differences are bound to occur that would produce a form of *stress* for the couple. The satisfactory resolution of these differences would necessitate compromise, which is usually possible. If the couple is raising a family, the compromising would probably continue until the children are grown. When the *stress* of parenting ends, it is possible, and likely, that *stress* resulting from the need to be individuals, in an environment in which the couple has become accustomed to compromise could take hold with disastrous consequences for the marriage.

Many of the *stresses* that are experienced during married life occur without any consideration of the reactions they produce and our abilities to deal with them successfully. Dealing with family members, trying to give equal love and care to more than one child are major requirements. So too are sharing love and quality time appropriately between spouse and children; maintaining a satisfactory (according to choice) level of existence and meeting financial commitments are also *stress*-producing events that are experienced daily, without concern about the levels of *stress* produced by these events. Other things also contribute to the *stress* situation in married life. Monitoring a child's physical and intellectual development; experiencing joy at children's successes, and sorrow when they fall short of expectations (with emotions that must be hidden from the children) all have the capability of producing severe *stress* in their individual lives.

Just as with financial *stress*, many of the current activities designed to remove *stress* are not capable of providing freedom from marital *stress*. Relaxation and decompressing will assist in reducing the need to utilize *stress* readjustment energy, and provide for temporary relief. But during each day the pressures of married life persist. Unless the couple is made aware of the heavy pressures they must endure, and unless they receive assistance in dealing with these pressures, there is a risk that the marriage would crumble and could bring along other potentially more dangerous *stress* situations for the couple, the children, relatives and friends.

Even when marriages appear to be successful, the individual partners have to deal with *stresses*, some of which could be produced by the success of the marriage. Especially in western society, the need to know that you are able to give and receive love can produce significant *stress*. In the fast paced world of today, many of us grow to become complacent about our actions. Quality time for spouses (and families) is something that might not be given a very high priority. It often demands special effort and the juggling of priorities to ensure that some time is available for the couple. Often one spouse might not be certain that the other's actions are the result of the love they share. They know that the possibility exists that their individual actions may be the result of habit, rather than acts of continuing love. If this should occur, there is the possibility that one, or both, partners might seek out experiences to regain confidence in their abilities to give and receive love. Unfortunately, in many instances these experiences are sought outside the marriage with disastrous consequences, and especially, the *stress* of guilt. The spouse finds it difficult to justify their actions and impose greater blame than necessary on her or himself. Their self-imposed shame might not permit them to recognize that the love experience that was being sought was the expression of a need to experience love with their married partner, and crippling *stress* becomes a dangerous possibility. This might be the source of the talked about "seven year itch."

We must also remember that the partners are people who would also be experiencing other *stresses* at the same time that marital *stress* affects their lives. Workplace, social, health, financial and other *stress*-producers are also being experienced and force the utilization of *stress re-adjustment energy*, that could be partly responsible for any weakness that might encourage the seeking of love reassuring experiences outside their marriage.

It is important, that couples be questioned directly about their reactions to various *stress* influences in their lives, if they are going to be assisted in making the determination of whether to continue, or abandon their marriage. As is the case, with the questions about workplace *stresses*, the individuals must be assured that there are no correct or wrong answers, but only honest ones.

Some questions that should be asked of themselves by the individuals, and by anyone providing assistance to the individual, or couple to assist in dealing with marital *stress*:

Are you dissatisfied with the institution of marriage?

Is there, currently, anything in your marriage that you consider satisfying?

When was the last time you could remember being happy in your marriage?

Could you identify the time (period), when you consider that things began to change?

Can you identify some of the other events occurrences in your personal life, at that time?

Do you know of anything unusual that was going on in your spouses' life at that time?

Would you want to continue in your marriage, if you could feel comfortable and happy with your spouse again?

Do you accept any responsibility for your current situation?

What is your perspective on the reason for your current situation?

Are you experiencing any frustrating or annoying events in your life that may not be related to your marriage situation?

Do you know, or suspect that your spouse might be experiencing situations that might be producing stress for him/her?

Is there anything that you continue to enjoy in your relationship with your spouse?

How much of a social life do you have with your spouse outside your home?

What is the most annoying event in your relationship at present?

What is the least annoying event in your relationship at present?

Is there anything satisfying in your relationship at present?

Have you communicated your feelings to your spouse?

Would you agree to meet with your spouse and a counselor, or friend to discuss your relationship?

Is your marriage a situation that you would choose to continue?

Have you set a deadline for improvement in your situation?

What is your spouse's take on the current situation?

What do you want (expect) from your marriage, at this time?

Are you aware of any outside motivating circumstances that promote, and/ or perpetuate your current dissatisfaction with your marriage relationship?

Could you list the things that annoy you about your relationship, at present?

Could you rate the things you have just listed according to the Stress Rating Scale provided?

Could you repeat the last exercise for the things you are happy about, at present?

Questions like these, and others that could be generated from responses would help the individual(s) to focus on their relationship in a controlled and sober fashion. They could point to areas of satisfaction and enjoyment that could be followed, and to areas for which a concentrated effort should be directed, in order to improve the relationship, if possible, or to a joint decision to adjust their current status for a trial period, and even permanently, perhaps.

Without this kind of introspective inquiry by the individual partners, and perhaps, a collective soul-searching of the issues to unearth the types of pressures in their lives, a final decision on their situation would be made in a vacuum. By learning to rate their *stress* reactions to each troubling situation in their lives, they could learn about those things that they could, each handle, individually and collectively. They could also begin to understand those things that they either have to work on together, or to accept, for togetherness; or to reject and choose a change in status.

Individuals and groups react differently to different types of *stress*-producing events

Each of us will react differently to the same level of any particular type of *stress*. We can all attest to this through recognition that different individuals have different pain thresholds. We know, too, that different individuals react differently in the face of large debts, and that different individuals have different levels of resistance to different diseases. Some of us will be extremely capable of resisting a certain type of *stress*, and, at the same time, be extremely submissive to a different form of *stress*. This would be apparent when an athlete such as a physically fit baseball player is terrified of spiders, but unafraid of being struck by a baseball thrown at speeds of over 90 mph from less than 70 feet away. Sometimes, our reactions to positive *stress* produce unbearable situations that overwhelm us—such as fainting upon hearing that one has won a contest. Some of us will be scared of facing a baseball thrown at a rapid pace from a short distance, some of us have no fear of spiders; and some of us will be unmoved, while some might be boastful, on learning we have won a contest. These things testify to the different ways in which different individuals react to different types of *stress*.

Stress, however, does not confine itself to our existence as individuals. Institutions, companies, racial and religious, as well as age and interest groups also experience forms of collective *stress*. Particular jobs also carry different types of collective *stress* experiences as integral parts of the jobs. Military personnel engaged in a war; doctors in a trauma unit, firefighters, police and other groups of employees all experience collective *stress* outside of, and concurrently with, their individual situations. We associate "burn out"—actually a form of *stress* failure reaction—to particular types of jobs. We frequently link group actions to racial and religious origins and their reactions to certain events, and to interpretations of events. These things happen because group *stresses* tend to stimulate group reactions.

The human race, as a collective whole, is also exposed to forms of group *stress*. The entire (at least a majority) of the race must endure the intrusive ability of television that forces us to be exposed to pressures caused by news broadcasts that dwell on conflict; contradictions, confusion; despair; destruction, and crimes of all sorts. Similar experiences intrude into our consciousness through movies, plays, books and newspapers. We exist under a constant threat of destruction by nuclear, chemical and bacteriological weapons; and mismanagement and destruction of our environment threatens to destroy our life support system. In addition, we live with the reality of possible natural disasters such as, earthquakes, volcanoes, tornadoes, hurricanes and other destructive weather patterns that can launch horrific destruction amongst us. Although we might react as individuals to these forms of global *stresses*, it does not rule out the possible existence of forms of collective responses by the human race.

Some common group *stresses*

Children, as a distinct group, face the *stress* of peer pressure, and parental pressure for them to succeed. Some students succumb to the *stress* of examinations, while others find writing exams to be a task which is accomplished without significant stress. Professional athletes, movie stars, music performers are under constant pressure to perform which causes constant *stress* each time they perform.

Stress could sometimes produce undesirable behavior in distinct groups

Just as *stress* could produce irrational, erratic and undesirable behavior in individuals, it could also have similar effects on distinct groups. We see this often, when special interests groups gather to protest some activity that is considered to violate human rights and needs. Activities that should have been completely peaceful, sometimes turn into ugly confrontations, which might be traced to a group *stress* condition.

In a multifarious country, as Canada, where several races and cultures attempt peaceful and democratic co-existence, group *stresses* sometimes cause accusations of racism. It is true that some individuals are racist, and that some groups include individuals who practice racist policies that lead to racially motivated actions against specific groups. However, all the activities that are considered, and challenged as racist ones, may not be the products of racism and could be the results of a form of *stress* that even the individual, or individuals carrying out the activities are unable to identify and understand.

Having to deal with other types and levels of *stress* could, sometimes, be responsible for unethical actions committed by police against identifiable minorities. It is quite possible that the individual (s) responsible might even think that their actions are motivated by racial differences, without understanding how other *stress* has contributed, or is contributing to the activities. Consider a police officer, whose home life is in disarray because of the time and risk that is necessary for the carrying out of his, or her duties. Imagine that the *stress* of police work is causing a rift in the family relationship, and one evening when the partners have planned some quality time together, the officer is called out to deal with a criminal situation. The officer knows that the partner is going to be annoyed, and may even be annoyed too. Arriving on the scene, the partner learns that the person who is believed to have committed a crime is a member of a minority group. It is a minority group who, rightly or wrongly, has been tagged as one that generally is involved in criminal activities. The officer may feel some anger at the disruption of the evening with his partner. The officer could be concerned and under *stress* because the job demands might cause additional and immediate family *stress* to occur on his return home, and possibly long-lasting *stress* in the days and weeks to follow. The result could be that the anger would be taken out on the individual who is assumed to have committed the crime that had disturbed his/her plan for an evening of adjustment or reconciliation. Members from the minority group, and the press are almost certain to raise the issue of racism. Even though the officer did not act out of racial hatred, and although his/her, actions did have some connection to the minority status of the supposed criminal, the action would have been caused by anger over the *stress* produced by a family situation. Though, technically, a response with some connection to race, it would not have been conducted because of the race of the individual being investigated.

At the same time, for the individual from the minority race, any tendency to be involved in criminal activities could be caused by social *stress* conditions. Having to exist in a society where there are fewer lawful opportunities for financial progress, and where the conditions of existence are considered to be less than equal to those for the majority produce considerable group *stresses*. In addition, the television, movies, books and newspapers, through the power of advertising, constantly reminds the members of the minority of the "good" life that they cannot participate in, and fuel anger hatred among the group. These *stresses* could result in making a life of crime appear to be the only viable alternative.

Success is possible even when facing severe *stress*

The fact that people, as individuals and groups, must face *stresses* in their lives, does not mean that *stress* is bad for you, nor that you should try to avoid *stress*. Despite the many *stresses* we face every day, many individuals and groups have shown that we can have successful lives despite the severity of the pressures we must endure. Dr. Hanson, in his book "Joy of Stress", points to the triumph of

Sir Winston Churchill, during the Second World War, as an example of triumph over extreme *stressful conditions.* Recently, we have examples of individuals who are physically handicapped, who conduct remarkable feats of endurance. One of the leading scientific minds of the last century is a person with physical handicaps. We have examples of athletes, as individuals and groups who have achieved levels of success that were considered impossible. Today, the computer and robotics permit several individuals to achieve levels of success in their lives despite various disabilities. Around us, we could observe that success is possible despite severe *stress* conditions.

The important thing about human stress is that just as we do for inanimate materials, we must learn to understand how we react to the different levels and types of *stresses* that confront us every day of our lives. It is only through this understanding that we could guard against being taken to the point of *distress* before we attempt to obtain relief from difficulties that accompany the experiences of *stress* in our lives.

Attempts to quantify *Stress* are erroneous

It is easier to deal with things, if we could assign a numerical value for the purposes of comparison. I believe this use of numbers to express different levels of activities has led to an effort to quantify *stress* in a general (universal) way, which is actually erroneous. The error is understandable, especially if we have made an error by regarding excessive *stress* (*distress*) to be simple *stress,* which does not, necessarily lead to impaired function, illness and possibly death.

Excessive *stress* is really the net result of a series of different types and levels of *stressful* experiences that we may be exposed to at the same time. Each different type of *stress* results in different levels of reaction from each individual. However, when the total *stress* effect on our bodies take us to a point where our abilities to react at a level that would re-establish homeostasis are limited, we reach a point of *distress* that could have harmful effects on our lives. While we are unable to predict the exact nature of this harmful effect, it produces activity that could be described, loosely, as a form of illness, but that illness cannot be successfully quantified for consistent application to all individuals. To quantify human reaction to *stress* by assigning numerical values that apply to all of us equally, incorrectly assumes that each type of *stress* affect each individual the same way, and that each individual's relative ability to react to particular types and levels of *stress* is exactly the same. It is an incorrect form of rationalization. Even though attempts are made to provide a measure of flexibility to account for differences in individuals this type of measurement is still erroneous. The technique still assumes that the variety of *stressful* events (which usually exists in different combinations and varying levels, for each individual) would act as a sort of equalizing factor for the determination of the final weight value.

Our personalities might dictate our abilities to respond to different *stresses*

If we are each born with distinct personality traits, as Dr. Taylor Hartman, suggests in his book, "The Color Code", then it is more likely that we are individually programmed to respond in individual ways to different types and levels of *stress*. Our DNA, fingerprints, voices and other body features are all different, so there is no valid reason to believe that our reactions to different *stresses* are all the same. This does not mean that we are limited by birth to react, forever, in the same manner to different types and levels of *stress*. As we grow from childhood to adulthood, we react differently to pain, and things like fear. We react differently to financial and social pressures. So it is quite possible that behavior modification, environmental conditioning, and other factors within our direct control could impact on our abilities to withstand *stresses* as we experience life.

We know from experience that someone who fears fire could be eventually trained to walk on hot coals; that persons who fear large bodies of water can be taught to swim and to withstand the *stress* of swimming in an ocean, where drowning is a possibility. Dr. Hartman, expresses a similar point of view concerning the human ability to change approaches to deal with different situations. He writes about becoming a "charactered" person by adopting characteristics of a different personality type to supplement our own, different personality type. The combined characteristics provide a strengthened character for dealing with situations (*stresses*) for which our natural personality types might not be ideally suited. If we are each different and respond to different types and levels of *stress* in different ways, then attempting to devise quantifiers for different *stress*-producing influences that could be applied universally would be erroneous, and would reflect certain biases.

Existing *Stress* scales are suspect

As suggested, previously, experts appear to have focused on human *stress* at the level at which it has already become *distress*, when they discuss what is, commonly, referred to as stress. What is commonly called stress is really the total result of our efforts to deal with the many *stress* experiences that affect our lives at any particular time. This effect is more noticeable, because it occurs at a point where we have used up all the energy that is naturally available to us for re-adaptation to restore homeostasis to our body systems. At this point (the **SREL**), the extent of chemical and biological changes in our bodies are readily observed to provide the common symptoms of Dr. Selye's General Adaptation Syndrome. I suspect that it is this syndrome that appears to have led to the consideration of *stress* as a singular illness, which has led, in turn, to the attempts to quantify *stress* by assigning numerical weight values to certain *stress*-producing events in our lives. People are asked to total the assigned points in order to determine *stress* levels being experienced, and to use these values to forecast the possibility of illness as a result of *stress*. One conclusion that could be drawn from this type of exercise would be that *stress* always results in death—which is also the assumption that is portrayed by Dr. Selye's GAS. It would be a wrong conclusion. Sometimes the effects of too much *stress* might produce gambling and theft, in the case of financial *stress*, and anti-social behavior in the case of social *stress,* and other types of reactions could be identified in the case of different types of *stress* experiences.

Any form of exercise to determine a set value at which *stress* would cause illness for all individuals incorrectly assumes that we are each affected to the same degree by any particular type of *stress*, and that each individual's relative ability to withstand a particular *stress* is exactly the same. It is a type of assessment that ignores the significance and impact of individual differences in our lives. We do not all die after the same length of illness because of cancer. We do not all feel the same effect from a severe case of influenza, and we do not all have to wear the same amount of clothing for comfort in the face of winter and summer temperatures. We can point to many other *stress*-producing events, and the different needs of individuals for personal comfort in dealing with them.

An examination of two notable scales: (Holmes-Rahe; and the Hanson Scale of Stress Resistance.)

The Holmes-Rahe scale is an accepted yardstick for human *stress* evaluation. This scale lists over 40 life events and it contains an allowance for miscellaneous events not included in the scale. While the scale attempts to permit some degree of flexibility to allow for individual differences, by suggesting that individuals place their own numerical values for the events listed on the scale, it contains a built in error that causes significant errors. The individual values given, are to fall within an arbitrary set of measurements that are used to indicate the relative importance of the events in each individual's life. It is also a scale based on western values that may be different to the values of people from other parts of the world.

As Dr. Hanson has attempted to combine his scale with the Holmes-Rahe scale, I present below some of the events listed in the Holmes-Rahe Scale, as they appear in Dr. Hanson's book, "The Joy of Stress", on pages 47 to 49.

Life Event	*Value*	*Your score*
Death of a spouse	100	__________
Divorce	73	__________
Marital separation	65	__________
Retirement	45	__________

Sex difficulties	39	__________
Change in number of arguments with spouse	35	__________
Mortgage over one year's net salary	31	__________
Trouble with boss	23	__________
Mortgage or loan less than one year's net salary	17	__________
Christmas	12	__________

There could be some benefit to this type of assessment, if it were used regularly by individuals to chart changes in their assessment of the ratings given to different events at different periods in their lives when circumstances and intensity of the events change. However, it utilizes too many easy and biased assumptions to have real and lasting value in assisting individuals to understand their reaction to the *stresses* caused by these events. The scale does not assist anyone to develop the means to deal, successfully with any of the events. It is only a measure for determining whether you score suggests that you might be close to being ill.

There are many questions that should be asked about this type of scale. Would the effect of Christmas be the same for everyone so that its relative numerical weight with respect to the death of a spouse would always be twelve hundredth (12/100)? Would the death of a spouse be a significant or most important event, if the surviving partner married the other because of the individual's wealth, or age, or poor state of health? Would the death of a spouse be the most significant event, if the spouse did not provide the level of companionship of a son or daughter? What if the person is from a region where the impact of death is not similar to the impact in the western world, would it be worth 100 points? Would the relative weight for retirement be the same for someone who planned for it and was in a good financial position, compared with someone who did not plan for it and would be dependent on a small government pension?

The reality of different individuals being able to experience different levels of the same type of *stress*-producing influence, and to react differently to different types of influences that produce *stress*, suggests that assigning numerical ratings to *stress* for general application, cannot produce valid information. The ratings cannot allow meaningful decisions about the impact of *stress* in an individual's life. Use of this type of numerical rating scale is further compromised by the selection of an arbitrary total to be used as the indicator of the possibility of significant change in a person's health condition, as a result of *stress*. Even if the arbitrary values used in the scale happened to be a correct representation of the effect of *stress* on individuals, the fact that we are each different would suggest that when a figure of 300 might be a good indicator of impending health problems for one individual, a figure of 200, or 500 might be more appropriate for making a similar prediction for another individual.

In his book, "The Joy of Stress", Dr. Hanson refers to the Holmes Rahe Scale and states, *"If your total score is less than 150 units, you have a 30% chance of serious change in your health within the next year. Up to 300 units gives you a 50% chance."* He also states that more than 300 units give you an 80% chance. Dr. Hanson admits that the extent of the health effect depends on the individual, but he does not relate the effects of *stress* to the differences in individuals. Unless all individuals are exactly alike, and possess equal abilities in resisting *stress*, such "broad-stroke" conclusions based on arbitrary test scores cannot be valid, or reliable. Experience teaches us that different people could withstand different levels of the *stress* produced by cold temperatures, and we know that different people have different comfort levels when exposed to *stress* produced by warm temperatures.

Dr. Hanson gives positive points for good genetics and negative points for poor genetics in his scale. I doubt the effects of genetics would be the same for each individual, whether they are considered "good", or "bad." Every unstable home would not carry with it the same level of disturbance for each person who existed under this condition. Dr. Hanson's suggestion that every one should use his arbitrary number for the initial tabulation, which should then be fine tuned by individual adjustments of a few points up or down, still cannot provide for the effect of individual differences.

Direct coping mechanisms are more understandable for evaluating individual response to *stress*

Individuals would be able to relate directly to things like budget adjustments required to cope with financial *stress* that results from the need to pay off a loan, than they would relate to arbitrary numerical units assigned to *stress*-producing events. The adjustments to physical, social and financial activity, as a person copes with the effects of different *stresses* would be much more meaningful than arbitrary values that are not related to the conscious responses that individuals experience in *stress* situations. The chemical and biological responses in our bodies are far removed from our conscious reality, unless they result in detrimental health and social problems that cannot be identified by the weighted, arbitrary *stress* values. The direct coping mechanisms that we apply, such as: increased physical effort in the case of physical *stress*; budgetary restrictions in the case of financial *stress*, or physical inconveniences, as we experience the *stress* produced by illness are more understandable to the human consciousness.

The bias-free *stress* rating scale, based on the materials sciences principles, requires individuals to relate to their own interpretations of the effect and response that occurred based on actual *stress* situations that they have experienced. Numbers from one to 10 are used, but an explanation of the type of response is matched to different numbers. The choices are made by the individual, who is closest to the impact of their reaction to different *stress* experiences in their lives. The scale is also flexible, to permit individuals to use a scale from 1 to 1000, or 1 to 10,000, or even 1 to 1,000,000, based on the numbers they are comfortable with. It is a scale that would allow individuals to determine the level of reaction they believe they can withstand, comfortably, and it would help to alert them to situations where they are approaching their SREL, and may need outside assistance to prevent being taken to *distress levels.* This type of scale permits pro-active approaches to dealing with *stress* before it becomes *distress*, and it helps us to be continually, considering how we respond to different types and levels of *stress*. It encourages us to seek the understanding of how we are affected by *stress*, and the nature of our responses to particular *stress*-producing influences in life.

The study conducted at the Medical Research Council Common Cold Unit, in Salisbury, England, that was published in the August 91, New England Journal of Medicine used a technique similar to the one in the bias-free rating scale. The researchers reported that they calculated a numerical stress level for each volunteer by questioning them about such burdensome events during the previous year as: moving; being fired; changing jobs; having a child; getting an abortion; suffering a burglary, or experiencing a death in the family. This approach used in the study, moves towards the approach of the bias-free rating scale, but it would be less reliable because the questions are being answered for a counselor, or psychologist. Things like being fired, getting an abortion, burglaries, and deaths may not, all, be significant events in the lives of all the people being interviewed at that time, and the responses may be given without adequate thought. I am confident that when you question yourself and you are the prime overseer of the inquiry, that you would more likely be able to be totally honest about your reactions.

Possible link between personality, adaptation energy and human *stress*

Dr. Selye tells us that each one of us possesses a certain amount of adaptation energy that we use up in dealing with *stresses* in our lives. He believes that once that finite amount is used up, death would occur. This is evident in the graph that depicts his General Adaptation Syndrome (GAS). [Appendix 2, page 119]

While I agree that inanimate materials have a finite ability to withstand stress, I am convinced that Dr. Selye is wrong about a finite amount of adaptation energy in humans, which once used up results in death. Human experience tends to suggest that people might have access to a reserve amount of Stress Re-adjustment Energy (SRE) that can be tapped to provide a strengthened ability to withstand *stresses.* I believe that our SRE is used up in proportion to the level of *stress* that is being experienced at any point in time, until we reach our Stress Re-adjustment Energy Limit (SREL) that is similar to the Proportional Limit for inanimate materials. At this point, the reserve adaptation energy allows humans to continue to resist *stresses* but obviously this cannot continue forever, and failure would eventually result if the *stresses* persist and the individual is unable to withstand them.

Nevertheless, I agree with Dr. Selye that each one of us possesses a finite amount of "adaptation energy." What Dr. Selye calls "adaptation energy", I call re-adjustment energy! I consider the human body to be in a constant state of adaptation to a variety of *stresses,* which would not affect us in a negative way, until we become overwhelmed by the need to resist *stress*, and we are forced to make changes to the techniques utilized for adaptation. I believe that the amount of reserve re-adjustment energy available to any of us depends on our preparation and conditioning (mental, physical, emotional, social etc.) for the combination of *stresses* we are called upon to accommodate at any point in time. This would recognize that individuals, who experience similar types and levels of *stress, or different types and levels of stresses* would have individual amounts of reserve re-adjustment energy to draw upon, and would not exhibit failure in the same manner, nor as a result of the same level of total *stress.*

The reserve re-adjustment energy levels that we possess would also be available for use when we face *stresses* that are completely different from any that we might have experienced before. Space travel and external activity in space are examples of *stresses* that the body might have to deal with on a first time basis, for which previously untapped reserve re-adjustment energy would be utilized.

Comparisons of individual responses to *stress*

A single individual (A), might be required to utilize a significant amount of re-adjustment energy to battle exposure to cold weather. Another individual (B), having to face the same degree of exposure to cold weather might handle it without expending much re-adjustment energy. This is evidenced from the varying levels of protective clothing worn by different individuals during a spell of cold weather. The individual (A) however, may regard the death of an individual as a joyous event to be celebrated, because it signifies being called home to rest, with the "Father", and might not use up much SRE. On the other hand, individual (B), who is hardly affected by the cold weather, might be extremely saddened by the death of a friend, and may require substantial use of SRE to cope with the situation.

The author believes that we all possess some finite amount of SRE at any point in time. However, it is doubtful that this energy would be produced in the same amount each time we require this type of assistance. Our bodies, if they are properly maintained as finely tuned machines, would more likely, use up an adequate amount of SRE to establish homeostasis, including an amount of reserve SRE, if necessary. For the body to produce more SRE than required would result in a different form of unbalanced situation caused by over-reaction that, probably, would, itself, require readjustment.

There is the possibility that individuals, sometimes, convince themselves that their normal abilities are insufficient to withstand certain levels of *stress.* In this event, the signals transmitted could result in a sort of misuse of re-adjustment energy that might have some effect on the individual's emotional and physical health. This is probably the way in which fear or apprehension affects individuals.

Our reactions to certain events are likely to be results of our conditioning from experience, education, desires and faith in our own abilities – perhaps, also to our faith in a divine being. I believe that positive reaction to our environment and experiences could actually enhance the levels of re-adjustment energy that are available for our use to adapt to *stresses*—even though the amount of re-adjustment energy must have a finite limit for any individual at any given point in time.

Dr. Taylor Hartman's Personality Color Code

Dr. Selye believes that the amount of Adaptation Energy available to an individual is determined at birth. I am in general agreement with this idea; however, I believe that experience and environment can be utilized to improve or reduce the level of re-adjustment energy an individual is capable of utilizing at any particular time period. I was able to read Dr. Taylor Hartman's book, "The Color Code", and to discuss his ideas with him. Dr. Hartman believes that each of us is born with a particular "color code", which may be by accident or design. I believe this idea is consistent with Dr. Selye's idea of a set amount of adaptation energy at birth. However, Dr. Hartman's concept also sees an individual being able to alter the manner of behavior in a given situation, despite the original color code, by becoming a "charactered person", through the adaptation of the personality of another color code to suit the situation. Dr. Hartman's idea conforms to my idea of individuals being able to modify re-adjustment energy levels on the basis of experiences, environment, education and personal philosophies.

Dr. Hartman contends that each of us is born belonging to one of the four Personality Color Codes (red, blue, white and yellow) that he has identified. Although he admits that none of us might ever be 100% of one of the color codes, he suggests that one of the four types will always be predominant. The dominant color is seen to dictate the motives needs and wants that make up our "Personality Profile"; and we are usually designated according to the two colors that show up the most in the results of our Personality Overview test scores. We would be designated Red/Blue, or White/Yellow, or Blue/Red. I have known several individuals, who have taken this test, and they all have claimed that the results were consistent with their own view of their personalities. I was given permission to reprint the "Personality Overview" chart, from pages 21 and 22 of the book, "The Color Code", which appears as follows.

	RED	BLUE	WHITE	YELLOW
MOTIVE	Power	Intimacy	Peace	Fun
NEEDS	To look good (academically) To be right To be respected Approval	To be good (morally) To be understood To be appreciated Acceptance	To feel good (inside) To be understood To be respected Acceptance	To look good (socially) To be popular To be praised Approval
WANTS	To hide insecurities (tightly) To please self Leadership Challenging adventure	To reveal insecurities To please others Autonomy Security	To reveal insecurities To please others Protection Contentment	To hide insecurities (loosely) To be noticed Freedom Playful adventure

Previously, I indicated that, Dr. Hartman, wrote about being a "Charactered Person". He was suggesting that, when it is necessary to deal with a situation that is best handled by being appreciated rather than being respected, a person who fits into the Red color would adopt the characteristics of the Blue color, for dealing with that particular situation. The yellow color would be selected, if praise was being sought.

Human reactions to events may be linked to the impact on our motives, needs and wants

It appears logical that our conscious reactions to *stress*-producing events in our lives would be dependent on the way in which we interpret the events to impact upon our motives wants and needs. It is this interpretation that would cause our anxiety, produce adrenaline, and, probably, trigger the adaptation response when we perceive the situation to be outside our immediate control. This would suggest the probability that our adaptation energy resources are influenced by our personality profiles.

If we consider an individual to be driven, solely, by the "power" motive (as discussed by Dr. Taylor Hartman in his Color Code), it is conceivable that should the individual be required to behave in a manner that displays power and authority, it would require little use of re-adjustment energy. On the other hand, someone whose primary motive is "to be good morally", might have to draw on reserve re-adjustment energy resources to function successfully in a situation where power and authority are required for successful completion of the task, or duty. In like manner, someone whose motive is "power" might require significant use of re-adjustment energy reserves when faced with a task or performance that requires a personal, more sensitive approach.

The amount of adaptation energy needed for any individual, in response to particular levels of *stresses*, would probably be determined by the degree to which that person has become a "charactered" person. It would depend on the ability to, successfully, blend the motives, needs and wants of the other personality colors into the pattern formed by the individual's dominant personality color code. This way, our personalities would have a direct bearing on the manner in which react to situations.

The author cannot vouch for the correctness of Dr. Hartman's idea of four different "personality color codes" into which all individuals are born. However, his idea of different personality color codes is consistent with the reality of human individuality and is one way in which we could probably explain why different individuals react differently to changing types and levels of *stress*. There is also the added similarity between Dr. Hartman's ideas, and those of Dr. Selye, who speaks about each individual being the recipient of a certain level of adaptation energy.

Differences between stress in materials and *stress* in humans

People are different from materials! While there may be (are) similarities between the way materials react to stress, and the manner in which humans respond to *stress*, there are significant differences that must be considered. These differences appear to give humans an advantage in dealing with *stress*.

Human machinery is superior to manufactured materials and machinery

In the book, "Stress without distress", Dr. Selye refers to the human system as "human machinery." It is an appropriate description; however, from an engineering technology standpoint the human body is more complex and closer to perfection, than any manufactured system. The human body consists of a skeletal structure with a degree of strength, flexibility and ability to be repaired that could not be duplicated in man-made structures. This human frame is capable of physical adjustment as our bodies grow to maturity and then becomes a lasting structural framework that withstands all the physical *stresses* that may be imposed on it throughout our lifetime. The body is blessed with a perfect electronic messaging system for transmitting and receiving signals that control our responses to meet diverse requirements, and which can generally withstand interference *stresses*. There is a closed loop water supply type system of heart (pump) veins and arteries that must deal with the *stress* requirements of supply and demand continuously, including periods of shutdown for repairs. There is also a waste disposal type system involving our intestines and other body parts that must cope with *stresses* resulting from the functions of intake, processing, storage and energy transfer, and then outflow. The human brain, unlike a computer that (up to now) does one thing at a time at an extremely high rate of speed, has to cope with the *stress* of managing a number of activities at the same time. The brain is a system possessing a power that man is yet unable to fully comprehend and utilize. There is also a human optical system that far exceeds anything man could produce.

Many other comparisons exist that would identify the human body as a superior piece of machinery, when compared to any manufactured material or machine. It is a fact that the human machinery is called upon to resist a number, and different types and levels of *stresses* at one and the same time, which makes *stress* analysis of humans a much more complex exercise than the stress analysis of materials.

Human emotion as *stress* producer

Perhaps the most significant area of human *stress* is the one that deals with human emotions. It has no parallel in the world of materials sciences! Every human emotion brings *stress* along with it. Excess of a single emotion, and/or *stresses* produced by a combination of emotions occurring at the same time, produce the greatest difficulty for analysis. The positive, joyful *stress* that results from the emotions that follows a promotion at work may have to co-exist with negative, sadness *stress* that results because a close family member is experiencing a drug, or alcohol related, or other problem at the same time. At that same time, other *stress*-producing influences may also be present in the form of a tight budget because of an increased mortgage rate, which might be happening at the same time as marital *stress* or some other form of *stress*. The individual must also cope with the normal daily *stresses* that life produces for us. These many, and varied types of *stresses* that affect humans, continuously, defy the kind of exact measurement that engineers utilize when dealing with inanimate materials.

Different types and situations of *stress*

The possibility of many *stress*-producing different behaviors occurring at the same time also suggests that consideration of the biological, chemical and other human responses to be indicative of a single condition called *stress* to be erroneous. If an individual experiences several *stress* events, simultaneously, which event would be treated? The single, most critical, event signaled by the biological, chemical and other bodily responses is more likely the onset of *distress*. It would still be necessary, and certainly most helpful, to identify the types and levels of *stresses* that produce the *distress* that an individual is experiencing. This type of recognition or, at least, the attempt to identify separate conditions, in combination with a bias-free measurement scale could benefit the approach to treatment. It could lead to the development of coping techniques to reduce the effects of the most critical *stress*-producing events in order to reduce the level of SRE needed to deal with the situation that exists at the time.

In the materials sciences and engineering, we recognize that different types of external loads produce different types of stress in materials. The stress is described as positive, or negative, based on the manner in which the top and bottom layers of the material are bent. Sometimes materials experience stresses in combinations, and sometimes, such as when the wind direction reverses itself, materials experience "stress reversal" where the type of stress changes from being positive to become negative. In engineering, it is possible to combine materials—such as concrete and steel—to take advantage of the strength properties of the individual materials (this might be similar to the adopting of the characteristics of a different color code to respond to particular situations). There are also techniques that could be applied to improve a material's ability to resist stress (this might be similar to improving life styles in order to improve one's ability to resist *stress*). However, regardless of similarities, no material would ever have to resist the differing number of *stress*-producing influences that the human body might have to withstand at the same time, and continuously.

In human *stress*, beneficial and pleasing influences, and those that aid in human development, such as physical exercise to build muscles, would be considered as "positive" *stress*. Non-beneficial and unpleasant influences, and those that harm rather than develop muscles such as torture, overeating and inactivity would be considered "negative" *stresses*. It is important to understand that "positive" *stress* carried to excess levels could also produce a *distress* condition. We may enjoy eating (which produces "positive" *stress*), but eating too much is detrimental to our health. We may enjoy soaking up the sun on a warm beach, but too much exposure to the sun is detrimental.

Despite the, generally, more *stressful* environment that men and women exist within, humans have a decided advantage over materials in internal resistance to external *stress*. Humans are able to make adjustments to environment, philosophy, life-style, thought patterns and even to modify their "personality profiles". We are also able to call upon professional and non-professional help to supplement existing natural and adaptation *stress*-resisting energy in dealing with different types and levels of *stresses*.

Stress combinations and reversals in humans

While stress combinations in materials could be pre-determined to allow for design modifications to allow a material to successfully resist external stress, the combinations for people cannot be pre-determined with complete certainty. Some of the everyday *stresses* are known, and they depend on the individual's daily needs, habits and preferences. Other *stresses* that occur because of situations or environments that cannot be pre-determined nor controlled are unknown and unpredictable in most instances. Only if it were possible for an individual to keep a complete and certain record of the types and levels of *stresses* that occur on a daily basis, would the predictability of behavior under certain *stress* combinations be possible. The bias-free *stress*-rating scale that is being advocated, encourages behavior to keep a conscious (and possibly written) record of an individual's reaction to different types and levels of *stresses* that have been experienced, but it could not predict reactions to unknown experiences. It should, however, provide information of the types of *stresses* that create difficulties for the individual. The combinations of different types and levels of stresses in materials produce one resultant combined stress effect. The combinations in human life also result in a total effect produced by the extent of the *stresses* being experienced at the same time. Therefore the behavior of materials and people could be considered to be similar.

Stress reversals in humans would be different than reversals in materials, but its existence should be acknowledged. There is no certain way of measuring when these reversals occur in humans, but we could envision some situations that would produce an effect that is similar to the development of stresses in materials when the direction of the wind changes. The joyful *stress* experienced by a child's success in school, might suddenly be turned into the sadness *stress* of learning that the student was involved in an altercation with a fellow student that results in a suspension. Or it may be the case of a spouse reveling in the victory of the partner's sports contest, who learns that the spouse suffered a crippling injury during the contest. The importance of recognizing the possibility of *stress* reversals in humans is warranted because we know from materials sciences that reversals weaken the ability of materials to resist additional external *stress* loads.

Individuals have different resistive capabilities for dealing with *stress*

The experience of different people having different reactions to temperature, and to the effect of some illnesses should alert us to the existence of different levels of resistance for different individuals. High debt *stresses* would not, normally affect someone who has been in and out of debt over an extended time period, as much as it might affect a salaried employee who has to deal with a large debt for the first time. However, the salaried employee might have a greater capacity for dealing with health *stresses* than the individual who is much more comfortable in dealing with high debt *stress*.

Quite possibly, it could be this difference in resistance capabilities to different types of *stresses* that might contribute to the success of some individuals, and the lack of success experienced by other individuals. If Dr. Taylor Hartman's assertions about personality color codes being imprinted at birth are true, then they might help to explain why different individuals choose different experiences that would expose them to different *stress* influences. The individual choices made by humans could be the result of the selection of influences, jobs and professions that are consistent with a person's motives, needs and wants. If individuals were fully in touch with their inner selves, they might be inclined towards choices that permit them to experience *stress*-producing events in which they experience positive enjoyment, and in which they would probably achieve satisfaction and success.

Although the money might alleviate the extent of the total *stress* that accompany participation in professional sports such as hockey, football, soccer or basketball, the physical *stress* may be pleasurable to those who choose these types of activities, but, the high level physical activity of these sports might tax the readjustment capabilities of other individuals. However, the *stresses* that might accompany participation in a world chess tournament would probably tax the readjustment capabilities of someone who is inclined towards the physical nature of some rugged sports. At the same time, there could be some individuals who would be quite comfortable experiencing the *stresses* of rugged sports as well as those of a highly mental contest such as chess. These individuals, in Dr. Taylor Hartman's scenario, would be individuals who have become "charactered" persons. They would have achieved the ability to handle both types of activities through the blending of another "personality color code" with their natural ones.

Despite the differences between materials and people and the difficulty of pre-determining *stresses* in humans, it should be possible for individuals to develop awareness of the manner in which they react to particular *stresses*. They would also be alert to the level to which they are affected while experiencing the combination of a number of identifiable *stress*-producing influences or events. An ability to access information about their reactions to *stress* conditions could help individuals to prepare themselves, through pro-active actions, to prevent being taken to extreme *stress* levels.

A significant difference between animate and inanimate material

One major difference between people and materials, when considering reaction to *stress*, is the human desire to perpetuate life. This desire to continue to exist allows people to make adjustments in order to cope with new experiences and/or the continuation of particular experiences. Materials have a fixed and limiting ability to resist stresses produced by various load combinations to which particular shapes and sizes of the material are exposed. Once a material part has been manufactured (there is an apparent difference in the case of properly produced and cured concrete that allows for increase in strength up to a certain amount of time) materials cannot improve, or change its stress-resisting capabilities. Humans, on the other hand, can utilize external support and lifestyle changes to improve abilities to resist *stress,* and the evidence suggests an ability to continue to resist *stress* even beyond the maximum level of *stress*-re-adaptation energy that we possess.

I doubt that Dr. Selye was exactly correct in his assumption that individuals possess a fixed amount of adaptation energy, which once used up cannot be restored. It seems more logical that the human system's adaptation energy could be recharged and improved through choices, and changes to lifestyle management. We are aware of individuals who hold on to life way beyond what is believed to be medically possible, and we know it is possible through resuscitation to restore life that appears to have ended.

Explanation of the author's *Stress vs.* re-adaptation energy curve

(A more detailed explanation of this graph is provided in Appendix 3, along with additional information about the stress vs. strain curve for materials for readers who might care to examine it.)

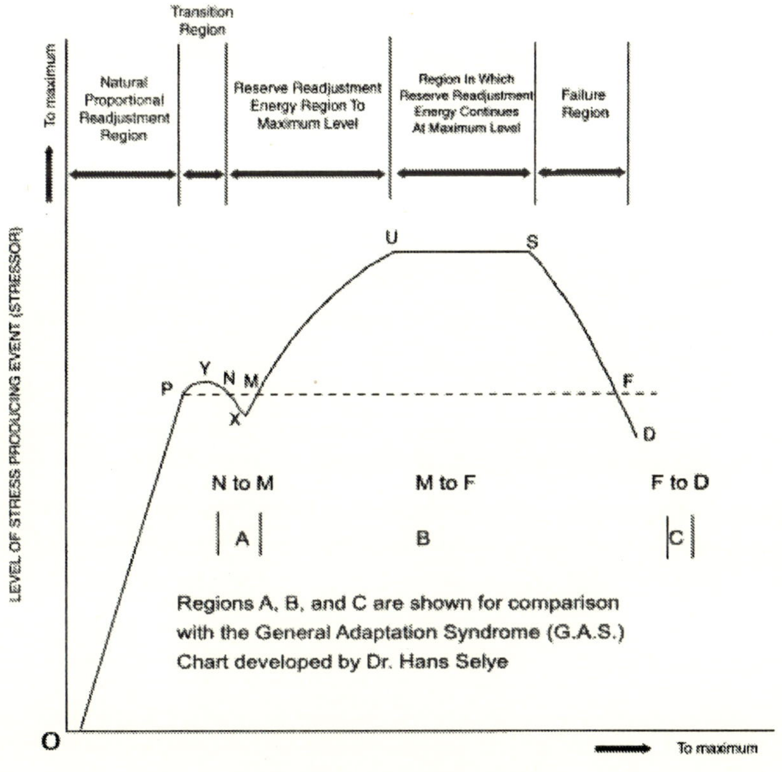

General considerations for shape of curve

For the determination of the shape of the curve of *stress vs. stress* re-adjustment energy, for humans, through use of the materials sciences principles, the curve is divided into five regions. This is different from the typical stress vs. strain curve for inanimate materials shown on page 122 of Appendix 2.

Natural, proportional re-adjustment region

The first region is named Natural Proportional Re-adjustment. The general consideration for the shape of the curve in this region recognizes that every experience in human life brings along *stresses*, which could rise to levels that threaten the natural human ability to maintain the body in a balanced state. It does not matter whether the experience is "positive" or "negative", the event would have an influence on homeostasis. When the body's balanced state is disturbed, the body would use up some of the available re-adjustment energy to re-establish the comfortable balanced state.

Normal re-adjustment energy, which exists in all humans, is utilized to counteract any particular *stress,* or combinations of *stresses*. It seems logical that the body would only utilize a sufficient amount of this energy to counterbalance the disturbing *stress* effect for as long as the body possesses enough natural SRE to effectively balance the effect of the *stress.* If the body were to employ more SRE than is required the body would be over-compensating, and it would produce its own unbalanced condition as a result. This suggests a proportional relationship between *stress* and *stress* re-adjustment energy up to a point (SREL) where the body reaches maximum ability to produce normal re-adjustment energy. This region, then, would be similar to the proportional region of stress vs. strain curves that have been determined in materials sciences and engineering.

The reaction in this region is similar to the situation where an elastic band is stretched and the increase in length is proportional to the pulling forces being applied. When this proportional relationship is plotted on a curve (see appendix 3) it appears as a line sloped (inclined) from left to right as the level of forces applied continue to increase. These inclined lines would be different for different individuals, and the amount of force that would end the proportional relationship would be different for different individuals. The point at which the proportional relationship ends is called the SREL (*Stress re-adjustment energy* limit).

This region for humans is similar to the region for materials where, should a stress, or combination of stresses be removed before the material reaches the end of the proportional relationship, the material returns to its original dimensions and would show no evidence of strain reaction. In the case of humans, the removal of a *stress*, or *stress* combinations before the SREL is reached, would allow the individual to return to the normal balanced state that would have existed before the detrimental effects of *stresses* affected it. This feature can be seen to be in agreement with the findings of stress researchers in the early 1970's.

Transition Region

Materials under stress also show a transition region. It is marked by the depiction of an apparent drop in the level of stress being experienced, which lasts for a short while before the stress levels begin to climb. Beyond this region, the rate of increase in strain resistance is faster in proportion to the external stress, than was evidenced in the proportional region for materials called the "Elastic Limit." A similar situation is exhibited in the diagram for *stress vs. stress* re-adjustment energy in the human body. A similar pattern is shown in the G.A.S. diagram devised by Dr. Selye. It could probably be understood best by the human reaction when attempting to avoid a dangerous and threatening situation. The sequence would be: (1) observation; (2) recognition of the danger; (3) fear response, and (4) flight, before development of a "second wind" to aid in continued flight which, if it continues could lead to exhaustion, and finally to collapse. It would be the fear response, and the initial flight, which demands a greater amount of re-adjustment energy before the body is ready to make the adjustment to overcome it, that would produce the effect of a falling level in re-adjustment energy.

The anxiety experienced by the body in this region is probably triggered by the knowledge that no adjustment has been made to provide additional re-adjustment energy to deal with the situation. It, probably, represents a delay in getting the signal through to the brain for the activation of reserve re-adjustment energy that is available to humans. In the case of materials that have only a fixed ability to resist external stress, the appearance in the typical stress vs. strain curve occurs because of an error in the calculation of the levels of the external stress. The stress is calculated by dividing the applied load(s) by the area of the cross section of the material that resists the imposed stress. At the time that the material reaches the proportional limit, there is a reduced diameter that is resisting the stress, therefore the stress values recorded during the experiments appear to be lower than the actual values. The full explanation for materials is beyond the scope of this book.

Reserve re-adjustment energy

After the transition region ends, the rate of resistance is shown to continue at an increasing rate up to a maximum value. In this region, the signals have been sent that activate the reserve amounts of SRE that is available to humans. Materials show a similar activity to the action in the curve drawn to depict the situation in humans. However, it is not because of an increased ability to resist external stress, it really depicts material that is capable of withstanding external loads beyond the proportional limit. In materials, the ability to continue to resist external loads continues along with an increasing rate of strain resistance until it reaches a point of failure called "Ultimate Stress". In one sense, the same is true for the human body, since the increased resistance continues to a definite maximum value.

Continuing re-adjustment energy at maximum level

The fourth region shown on the curve takes the shape of a horizontal line. This region is very different from any part of the typical stress vs. strain curve for any inanimate material. While the graph for materials curves upwards to a maximum value, at which point failure has occurred, then curves downward again to demonstrate the end of any strain resistance capacity, the graph for humans reflects the desire to perpetuate life that is associated with humans. It shows that humans would continue to fight against crippling *stress* at the maximum level for some time, before the body's system succumbs to failure from the effects of *stress.*

At this point in time, this region of the curve cannot be proven to exist. However, we know that it is difficult to predict exactly when life ends, and that in many instances, people could be resuscitated if action is taken quickly. We also know of some cases where people continued to live way beyond the time that medical science would have expected them to continue living, and it is this aspect of human life that is represented in this fourth region. It is also a region that resembles Region B, of Dr. Selye's GAS chart, even though this graph was prepared completely independent of Dr. Selye's work. This graph is similar to the graph for materials, but it allows for continuing resistance through re-adjustment energy for some period after the maximum level of resistance has been reached.

We could probably identify with the phenomenon depicted in the curve by considering a *stress* situation at a level below the maximum that a body can withstand. It would be the physical effort described as a "second wind" when suffering the effects of physical exertion that is associated with the running experience. It also occurs in other situations. We could probably remember an occasion when we might have felt completely drained and was ready to give up. However, if we persevered a little longer, from somewhere within ourselves, we discovered a source of energy to propel us on to achievements beyond the limits that could have been expected when we believed ourselves to be at the end of our energy capabilities. The renewed energy effort is probably the result of reserve re-adjustment energy, which would not last forever, and could still give out before we reach our goal, even when that goal might be within our sights.

The distance that our goal is located from the point at which our efforts to attain it begin, probably makes a significant contribution to the level of *stress re-adjustment energy* that would be utilized during the effort. If we should fail, when the goal is within easy reach, then failure could be considered to have occurred at a reduced level of *stress* than what is actually being experienced, because the level of external pressure should become less as we approach our goal. This might even be consistent with "fear of success".

The technique for plotting individual *stress* curves is discussed in Appendix 3. However it is not necessary to plot individual curves in order to determine your level based on the bias-free chart that is being promoted. Individuals could determine their *stress* levels based, solely on the definitions given for the different levels on the chart.

The need for a bias-free *stress* measurement scale

Throughout this book, suggestions have been made in support of the use of the proposed bias-free scale for determining individual reactions to different types and levels of *stresses*, and also to the combined effect of series of *stresses*. These suggestions have been drawn from consideration of the established methods for evaluating stress reaction of materials in order to ensure that the materials used for construction and manufacturing would not be exposed to levels of stress that would produce "failure". As a result of the materials sciences investigations of the ability of materials to resist external stress, engineers are able to design parts that would not be taken to failure on the basis of the level of stress produced by known external loads that produce stress in materials. The parts are also designed to handle maximum loading situations that could be predicted over the period during which the part is expected to be in use. The proposed scale could never achieve the certainty of the experiments conducted in the materials sciences. However, its use, over time, ought to provide individuals with a better knowledge of their ability to handle particular types and levels of *stress*, without being taken to the *distress* level and the resulting complications that would follow. The scale could also be utilized to predict ability to deal with combined *stresses*, if the scales are adjusted to higher values.

Any error that might occur because of an incorrect diagnosis of an individual's true situation when a *distress* or over-*stress* situation exists, is compounded by a failure to recognize each individual to be different, and to react differently to different types and levels of *stress*. As discussed previously, one person might be better at dealing with financial *stress*, than another person; but the other person might be much less affected by the *stress* produced by a medical condition. Some individuals might be able to handle marital *stress* easily, but may be unable to deal with *stress* produced on the job. Some individuals are more comfortable in cold temperatures, while others enjoy similar levels of comfort in the hot and humid weather. It is because we are different, that some would enjoy physical pursuits, while others would seek intellectual stimulation. Many other situations could be cited to show that we are each different, with different gene make-ups, and would therefore have different needs where SRE and SREL are needed to resist the effects of external *stresses.* These situations would be similar to the way materials react under different types of external load situations, based on their different strength qualities.

Several efforts are being employed to assist individuals to deal with *stress* conditions successfully. However, the individual needs do not appear to be seriously considered in the many group activities that are utilized. While these group activities may be able to assist in the physical and mental *stress* areas, and even provide some relief in the area of social *stress*, they do not appear to focus on a pro-active approach to preventing individual stress conditions. Even where a preventative nature is considered, the general type of cure does not address individual differences. This does not mean that current efforts are wasted! It would follow that if one, five or ten *stressful* events combined to take an individual beyond the SREL, then any effort that would reduce the need for SRE (even temporarily) would permit the individual to handle the remaining *stress* condition better. However, these methods do very little to help the individual understand what is happening, or to work on the development of lifestyle approaches that could prevent the external influences from producing high levels of internal *stress* in the future.

The type of generalized approach to the difficulties arising from human *stress* situations (including the efforts of experts), is the kind of response that leads to general advice of taking a vacation to reduce *stress* (as was given by Dr. Selye, in the book, "Stress without distress"). If the cause of an individual's *stress* problem(s) is a financial burden, then taking a vacation might aggravate the financial situation and would, probably, be the wrong remedy. If the cause of *stress,* or over-*stress* was a result of tension at work, a vacation might not work, unless the individual is someone who is able to refrain from thoughts about the workplace situation during the vacation. The possible failure to enjoy the vacation would only compound the issue, when the person returns to the workplace, and must face the same *stress*-producing conditions that necessitated the seeking of relief from them. We also know from materials sciences, that stress repetitions can cause failure of materials at even lower levels of stress than the material is normally capable of resisting. Perhaps the same would be true for humans.

We could be better off, if we could examine and analyze human *stress* from an individual standpoint, just as we evaluate the ability of materials to resist stress on the basis of the individual characteristics of each material. As in materials sciences, we need to find a way to assist individuals to determine their SREL for individual, and combinations of *stress* experiences. If we could do this, we could help individuals to guard against being taken beyond their SREL, without seeking assistance from professionals, and perhaps friends and family. This would require a *stress* measurement scale that would be free from bias such as: race, religion, gender, education, personal preferences, and other factors. It must be a scale that each individual could interpret based on their experiences. It should not be a scale where we assign arbitrary numerical values to particular events, without consideration of different conditions, inclinations and capabilities of each individual. We should note that when we visit professionals for assistance in dealing with *stressful* situations, they are not able to carry out a physical examination and cure us. The professionals respond to our interpretations and recollections of our experiences to assist us to find solutions that would permit us to cope with the situations we face. The core knowledge for any solution rests with the individual. Beneficial use of the bias-free rating scale would require a definite and continual attempt by each individual to identify and investigate the *stresses* we face every day, and this exercise, itself, should be helpful. The bias-free scale is a measurement device that considers, only, an individual's evaluation of his/her reactions to *stresses*.

One of the first things required, would be an understanding of the many things that cause *stresses* in our lives. It should not be necessary to pay particular attention to all of the influences and situations that we have ever experienced. Some of the experiences would have had a minimal effect on us, and could be eliminated from the exercise, initially. It is those situations that affect us noticeably, that we should be more concerned about. However, we should also be aware of the possible total effect of all *stresses* in our lives at any particular time, as the need for SRE could be increased as a result of minor *stress* events that occur at the same time as other significant *stresses* in our lives.

A partial list of common *stress*-producing events and influences

Attending school, college or university
Being successful
Being a failure (in the eyes of the individual)
Being a soldier on the battlefield
Being the person the soldier leaves behind
Being a policeman, or fireman
Being the spouse of a policeman, or fireman
Broken relationships
Change in careers while still relatively young
Change in careers while over 50

Coping with change
Coping with Christian ethic (Christian)
Coping with Christian ethic (non-Christian)
Dealing with bureaucracy
Death of a spouse, or lover
Death of a parent, son or daughter
Death of any family member
Debts, interest rates, stock reports
Driving on highways
Driving in the city
Driving to unknown areas
Fears
Frustrations with lack of influence in politics and business
Giving up smoking, or an addiction
Job search/interview
Job satisfaction/dissatisfaction
Job evaluation
Job transfer to different location
Loss of a job
Lack of funds for necessities
Lack of financial savings
Life in a crowd
Loneliness
Marriage, and marriage compromises
Medical illness (minor—common cold)
Medical illness (major – surgery)
Medical illness (extreme—AIDS, cancer)
Mortgage payments as a ratio of cash flow
Planning a trip or event
Phobias
Relationships with co-workers; family; friends, supervisors
Reading newspapers
Rent payments
Travel (daily commuting or vacations)
Viewing television news
Waking up to an alarm clock
Withdrawal from an addiction
Winning a lottery
Writing an exam

Worry about social conditions

Worry about the environment

Worry about being forced to work for welfare, or in positions for which one has not been trained

And many other situations we experience daily

Words that could be used to describe reactions to events and influences

As you think back to events in your life that produced a measure of *stress*, there are some words that could be used to describe your feelings. You could then assign a level from the bias-free scale to the feeling experienced for any event, where you feel certain about the way it affected you, and the way you reacted. By comparing the words with the event, you would also be developing an understanding of how you react to certain events. The following word list is not complete, and the words may be used in different forms from the ones listed here.

Positive words such as: appreciated; admired; accomplished; brilliant; comforted; elated; energized; fulfilled; joyful, justified; strong; successful, victorious and vindicated would identify positive experiences. They would be applied to events and influences with which you felt comfortable. Most of these words would, usually, apply to experiences that did not take you above your SREL, but, you should be aware that being overjoyed could sometimes produce *stresses,* which combined with other *stressful* experiences that are occurring at the same time, to take you to a distress level. The same would apply to any experiences for which a positive word or phrase is chosen to define your reaction. Therefore it is important to attempt to identify other situations that were occurring at the time any particular situation was relevant to your inquiry.

Negative words such as: angry; depressed, despised; afraid; hurt; jealous; numb; pitied; unfocussed, used and wasted would identify negative experiences. They would apply to situations that might severely tax your SRE, but may not advance you to your SREL. However, in combination with other *stressful* experiences, they could cause situations that take you beyond your SREL

You may not be able to identify the full range of *stressful* experiences that you might have endured at some past instance in your life, but you might be able to identify the critical events. In any event, the exercise should be directed to times when you felt certain that you experienced positive and negative effects of *stress.* In the case of individuals who are interested in developing understanding from the first day that you apply this rating scale to your life, the task would be much simpler if you would be able to concentrate on recent and current *stress* situations. However, even if you were working with a health professional, you would not be providing complete information, unless you are capable of remembering everything about some past moment in your life. You can only do the best that you can.

The bias-free *Stress* rating chart

It would be wonderful if a foolproof system could be developed by which each individual could record information that would alert them to the level of *stresses* experienced at any point in time, past and present. This type of information, if it were available would result in graphs of *stress* vs. re-adjustment energy that would be the equal of the stress vs. strain graphs for inanimate materials. The many differences observed in individuals, and the variations in the number and levels of *stresses* experienced daily do not permit a simple measuring device. At this stage, individuals must rely on honesty and recollections of the manner in which *stresses* and combinations of *stresses* impacted on their lives previously. In some instances, individuals would have to forget about past experiences and begin the exercise from this point on.

Dr. Selye states that, "*adaptability is probably the most distinctive characteristic of life*", and he also tells us that, "*not everyone is born with the same amount of adaptation energy.*" If we accept Dr. Selye's views, then it should be apparent that individual determinations of reaction to *stresses* are required in order to provide the most useful information about individual reaction to *stress.* Dr. Selye's views are consistent with the views of Dr. Taylor Hartman, who tells us that, "*personality is an interpretation of life*", and that, "*personality is a code of behavior.*" These views also appear to follow the materials sciences approach to materials as having individual capabilities to respond to external stress. The individuality of humans should be considered and reflected in any measurement of reaction to *stresses*, and it must be considered in developing methods of treatment and adjustments to assist individuals in dealing with *stresses.*

Engineers and materials scientists have an easier task

Engineers and materials sciences have an easier task in determining how materials react to stress, than medical experts have in the determination of human reaction to *stress.* Actual changes in dimensions and external changes in loadings that produce stress in materials can be easily calculated to predict the behavior of materials with a high degree of certainty. However, although it is possible to obtain measurements of chemical and biological changes in the human body during reaction to *stress*, it is still almost impossible to accomplish this on a continuous basis. It might be possible to employ virtual reality to recreate *stressful* conditions for measurement of human reaction levels through measurement of levels of chemical and biological changes, but it would probably be impossible to do this on a continuous basis.

If it were possible to examine individuals in a laboratory setting every time they experience *stress*, it would be possible to obtain exact measurements of reactions to various types and levels of *stress*. However, the more important requirement of knowledge about how individual and combined *stresses* affect them, would not be satisfied, and individuals would still be unable to determine when they are approaching limits of their abilities to respond to *stress*. It is this need that cries out for a pro-active approach when dealing with *stress*, so individuals could make timely decisions about seeking external assistance, or carrying out personal life-style management changes to avoid becoming *distressed*.

Individuals are alert to their reactions to various types and levels of *stress*

Individuals would normally be more alert to their actual feelings and emotions, as well as increases and decreases in physical capabilities during periods of *stress* both before and after any triggering of the General Adaptation Syndrome. A measurement scale that is based on personal interpretation of feelings and behaviors— under particular conditions of *stress* (both individual and combined)— would be more helpful. Such a scale should be better than any scale based on arbitrary values decided by someone who is in an observation situation that is remote from the actual behavior of the person experiencing the *stress*. This type of scale would permit the recording and charting of individual reaction to *stress* in a manner that might even be able to predict the conditions that would take someone beyond their capacity to react to a *stress* situation that is beyond their natural and normal capacity to respond.

Numerical ratings for the bias-free scale

STRESS RATINGS FOR INDIVIDUAL REACTION TO STRESS (© C.Preddie, P.Eng.)

RATING	LEVEL OF REACTION
[0]	NO APPRECIABLE EFFECT
[1]	EASILY HANDLED (*No apparent positive nor negative effects*)
[2]	MINOR DIFFICULTIES (*Required minor adjustments in habits, attitudes etc.*)
[3]	NOTICEABLE and MEASURABLE DIFFICULTIES (*Required major adjustments to habits and attitudes, or an extended period of minor adjustments*)
[4]	SEVERE DIFFICULTIES (*Required major adjustments for an extended period and/or adjustments in unrelated areas*)
[5]	EXTENSIVE DIFFICULTIES (*Required to make commitments and/or take actions that are contrary to personal preferences. May also experience fear of failure*)
[6]	CONTINUED EXTENSIVE DIFFICULTIES (*Situation is not completely resolved, or forced to continue beyond anticipated deadline. Situation may leave lasting scars and may affect behavior for a long time*)
[7]	ONEROUS EXTENSIVE DIFFICULTIES (*Situation still unresolved and produces noticeably changed behavior and attitudes as individual exhibits difficulty to cope*)
[8]	IMPOSSIBLE EXTENSIVE DIFFICULTIES (*Impossible to resolve by normal means acceptable to individual, Individual ex-*

periences detrimental physical, mental and/or emotional reactions that require external assistance to deal with situation)

[9] CRIPPLING EXTENSIVE DIFFICULTIES (*Individual is incapable of dealing with resolution; attempts avoidance and/or utilizes means of covering up failures. Individual is unable to cope*)

[10] ULTIMATE EXTENSIVE DIFFICULTIES (*Failure point is reached. There is lack of concern for self and others; exhibits escapist behaviors such as: alcoholism; drug use; irresponsible sexual activity, and things like high stakes gambling. Individual sometimes suffers permanent disability, and sometimes death may result*)

(The **SREL** might occur at levels 5 or 6 for most individuals.)

This Rating Scale differs from scales like Holmes-Rahe, where every individual is considered to have a similar reaction to types and levels of *stress*, even though the scale allows for some individual adjustment after the totals have been added. In Holmes-Rahe, for instance, the maximum stress producer for all individuals is considered to be death of a spouse, for which each individual should record 100 points. Under the bias free scale, each individual would be asked to select a level based on their personal interpretation of their reactions. Human *stress* analysis from a materials sciences standpoint would recognize that the death of an identical twin, or the death of a child who has provided companionship that was lacking in a relationship with a spouse, might cause the highest *stress* for some individuals. The motive for the marriage relationship, and cultural influences might also affect the level to be assigned for different individuals.

However, the bias-free scale is not designed to supplant the efforts of professionals. In fact, it would complement the work of professionals who assist people who are *stressed* to a point where they require assistance to deal with it. The selection of levels in this scale would depend on individual perception of the manner in which a particular type, or level of *stress*, or combinations of *stresses* affected the emotion, energy level, physical and medical well being of the person. This perception, except for individuals in some form of "denial", should be free of bias, and it should reflect individual ability to deal with *stress*, on the ability to adjust to *stressful* conditions that affect them.

Use of this scale also encourages timely, personal analysis of the effects of *stressful* conditions for an individual. Unlike the determinations, when visiting a professional counselor, which might be an after the fact rationalization, this scale permits on going, current evaluation. The most important benefit that might be derived from a commitment to utilize this scale, and sincere and honest on going analysis, is the preventative nature of the exercise. Proper and conscientious use of this scale could be of great benefit to each individual by allowing them to avoid continuing in a *stressful* situation that could become onerous and overpowering, before taking corrective action.

Although this scale extends from 0 to 10, different individuals could operate with a scale from 0 to 100; or 0 to 1000, or even from 0 to 1,000,000. In fact the use of higher values would facilitate the addition of the effects of several types and levels of *stresses* at the same time to determine the level of reaction under combined *stress* conditions. There is no need for perfection in utilizing this scale, and no one could prove you wrong in your personal judgment. It is the same personal judgment (without the numerical values) that you would take to a professional counselor.

We are the best people, who could determine how we react to *stress* in our daily lives. At this time, we may not be paying much attention to the way we respond to *stressful* situations. However, better than anyone else, we know how we are affected by, and how we react to medical situations, as well as such things as work difficulties, financial situations and emotional and social problems. The bias-free measurement scale gives us the ability to document our reactions in a measurable form, in order to develop a better understanding of ourselves, and the way we deal with life's *stresses*. We cannot escape from *stress* because it is a part of life. By itself, *stress* would not kill us, nor injure us, unless the *stress* is excessive, and we are incapable of dealing with it on our own. Better knowledge of ourselves and the limits of our abilities to deal with life's *stresses* would enable us to have better lives. If it were possible to measure (with absolute certainty) levels of applied *stresses* and the amount of **SRE** needed to handle different situations effectively, we should all be able to enjoy *stress,* without experiencing *distress,* as recommended by the late Dr, Hans Selye.

If an individual is alert, it should be possible to determine the situations at home, or at work, or in social settings, that tend to rile them and cause "crankiness" or some other form of negative type behavior. This kind of knowledge would assist them in protecting against outbursts that cause remorse and guilt, and the accompanying additional *stresses* that such emotions produce.

Possible use of this type of chart in business and group situations

As indicated in Appendix 3, use of the bias-free scale could be conducted through the use of graphs. This would be similar to some of the charts in use in business in the form of indices that indicate the financial health of a business venture. Therefore this type of rating scale, when made into a graph, could be utilized in business situations.

For businesses, a possible list of business stress-producing events might include the following:

Interest rates
Dollar value vs. US dollar
Debt level
Labor Market situation
Labor contract
Employment equity provisions
Trade regulations
Product market trends
Human Resources policies
Corporate policy
Government policies
Terminations policy
Technological change
Profit margins
Investment policy
Aging staff
Staff development
Others

Response rating scales that indicate how a business functions under an individual stress-producing event, or combinations of events could be developed to provide the same kind of information about reaction and response to stress, in a manner similar to that for human *stress.* This kind of information would be helpful in making business decisions. Different charts would have to be developed for each different business, and would not be useful for comparison with charts developed for different business enterprises.

There are distinct groups such as policemen, firemen, airline pilots, waitresses, teachers, nurses and some others, who are subject to particular *stressful* conditions experienced as part of their responsibilities. Situations that require the same type of responses from individuals in the groups could be identified as *stress*-producing ones that could be utilized in the same manner as those suggested for use in business situations.

How to use the bias-free *stress* measurement scale

In Appendix 3, you will be shown examples of the types of graphs that could be constructed for reading values of your *stress* reaction measurements. Graphing is a method that could be useful for readers who are familiar with information provided on graphs; however, the measurements could be recorded using numbers only. Whether you use the graphical method, or an exclusively numerical listing method, it is recommended that you try variations to the 1 to 10 scale that has been used by the author to explain his bias-free scale. Scales varying from 1 to 100, or 1 to 1000, or even 1 to 1,000,000 could be supplemented.

For a scale of 1 to 100, use values of 1, 10, 20, 30 ... 100. For a scale from 1 to 1000, use values of 1, 100, 200, 300 ... 1,000. For a scale of 1 to 10,000, use values of 1, 1,000, 2,000, 3000, ...10,000; and for a scale of 1 to 1,000,000, use values of 1, 100,000, 200,000, 300,000 ... 1,000,000. The numerical values represent individual **SRE** units, and the values chosen by one individual bear no comparison with similar values, if they were to be chosen by others.

In my definition of *stress*, I included a statement about homeostasis that indicated it would be related to a state that your body system "*has become accustomed to.*" It was indicated that this statement would allow for life style management changes. In a recent discussion with a friend, who had utilized my bias-free scale to evaluate her response to *stress*, she advised me that had she used the scale about 12 years ago, she would have been at level 8, or 9. At that time, she was dealing with a "messy divorce", and all the repercussions on herself and her family. When she spoke to me, twelve years after her divorce, she was a retiree, and one who was volunteering to serve part-time with a religious organization, and she considered herself to be at a level of 4, or 5. This might appear to suggest that individuals could return to lower reaction levels even after being *stressed* beyond their **SREL**, once life style management changes have been effected. This could be true, but I suspect that it reflects a difficulty with the use of the 1 t0 10 scale that might limit selection for individuals who may not be able to work with such low values for re-adjustment energy. This experience is a major reason for the recommendation to use higher values for your bias-free scale, especially when you use it for the first time.

An example of use of the bias-free rating scale

As most of us could relate to a financial debt situation, the situation chosen is for a debt of $1200.00 to be repaid in monthly installments over a period of one year (similar to the situation shown in Chart 1, in appendix #3.

Imagine a situation, where your monthly cash flow, after all expenses are taken care of, to be $120.00. Then, payment of about $100.00 per month to repay the $1000.00 loan could be handled without creating a significant financial *stress* situation. However, it might affect your ability to handle minor financial emergencies, should any arise. One individual might choose level "1" from the rating scale for this situation. At the same time, another individual, whose life experiences have encouraged the retention of a set amount of cash at all times for emergencies, might choose level "2" from the scale. Some other individual, facing the same situation, might choose level "3", based upon their approach to financial matters, and their personal confidence level with regard to job security and other relevant matters.

If the suggested situation, given above, did occur, and the individual was forced to give up going to the movies in order to pay off the loan, then the choice of level "2" would be more appropriate, since it would have required a "minor adjustment in habits". If the individual were disposed to play the lottery each week, and was forced to give up the habit, and the hope (real or false) of winning a large sum of money, then the individual might have selected level "3" to represent a "major adjustment to a habit." Level 3 might also have been selected if it meant playing the lottery one rather than four times each month, as an "adjustment for an extended period of time". Another individual might even choose level "4" for this situation, if it were considered a "major adjustment for an extended period of time in an unrelated area."

During the period that the loan is still being repaid, it is possible that a situation arise that forces the individual to find additional funds for an emergency situation. This might force the individual to incur additional debt—even from friends and family) to make the monthly payments and the selection might advance to level "5"on the scale. At this time, the situation would require a commitment to repay, and an action "contrary to personal preferences". After 12 months, if the loan was not completely repaid, the choice of level "6" because repayment of the additional money that was borrowed now renders the situation to be unresolved.

Should the situation continue beyond one year, and if the individual were forced to borrow from one person to pay another (such as to borrow from VISA to pay Master Card), the person might then select level "7", because of "noticeably changed behavior" and the "difficulty in coping". However, this same situation might cause another individual to select level "3", based on the way the individual responds to financial debt situations. We know that some individuals could be million of dollars in debt, and would feel quite comfortable in planning another financial venture that would require several more million dollars of debt. These individuals' reaction to financial debt would still fall under the same principles as one those who might be fazed by a $1000.00 debt, but the amount of debt to take them to their SREL would be much higher.

If the minor debt situation, that was originally being considered, could not be resolved by normal means (for the individual), it could force consultation with credit counselors, and perhaps mental and emotional reactions. Then level "8" might be an appropriate choice. And, should the situation result in the individual's refusal to open mail relating to the debt, in order to avoid having to deal with the matter, then level "9" could be the choice.

Finally, if the situation should result in social problems, such as broken friendships, or consideration of raiding a family member's piggy bank, failure would have occurred and level "10" should be chosen. Although ultimate failure would have occurred, the individual would still be alive.

A similar situation could be developed for an individual's reaction to the illness of a common cold, a migraine headache, or other forms of illnesses. Any illness would produce *stress* as individuals attempt to cope with the medical condition. In the case of the common cold, if the individual is able to perform customary activities at home, and at work, even though awareness of the cold is present, the chosen level may be "1". Should the cold be more severe, requiring absence from work, the level chosen may be "2" on the scale. If the cold necessitated a visit to the doctor, and a longer absence from work, the chosen level could be "3", or "4". If the cold progressed to a more serious illness, such as pneumonia, the level could be "5", or "6". The suggested levels could be higher, dependent on the age of the individual, and the degree of impact it produces on the person's life. We know that the simple cold could advance to level "10", which could eventually produce death.

A recommendation for a starting point

As it would be impossible to remember every *stress* experience of one's lifetime, it is recommended that each individual begin with current *stress* situations.

Identify each situation that that you perceive to be creating *stress* in your life, and choose a value of **SRE** units that you would assign to each. Do not expect your initial selections to be the final values you would choose as those that define the levels of your reactions to particular *stresses*. You may wish to adjust them, once you have become accustomed to use of the bias-free scale and become more comfortable with its use. On reflection, you may consider the effects of a particular *stress*, or combination of *stresses* to be out of line with some other selections you have made, which might necessitate readjustment in the values previously assigned. For example, initially, you may have considered a debt/income ratio of six (6) to have required 2500 SRE units; however, later you might recall a medical *stress* experience for which you had chosen a value of 2000 SRE units. But, on reflection, you consider the medical situation to be more taxing on your total body system than the financial *stress* experience. This would suggest that either the value for the debt situation should be reduced, or the value for the medical situation increased.

As the values of SRE units chosen would represent individual preferences, you could actually begin by assigning arbitrary values to different types of *stresses* that you have experienced. For example, under medical *stress* you could assign values such as: migraine (3000 SRE units); common cold (500SRE units); minor operation (1000SRE units). At the same time, for debt *stress*, you may choose the following: debt to income ratio 1:2 (1000SRE units); for ratio 4:1 (4000SRE units). For the social *stress* of dealing with children's successes or failures, you may assign a value of 1000 SRE units. Later, as you focus in on your reaction to individual *stress* experiences, you may want to adjust the values you chose previously. It would probably take a while to obtain results that you are totally comfortable with, but the exercise should prove to be rewarding, as you develop awareness and expertise in the introspective analysis of your reaction during periods of *stress*. The goal of your efforts should be to become comfortable with the values you assign for SRE units used in your reaction to various *stress* influences that you are able to identify. By attempting to get in touch with your feelings and emotions while you experienced particular *stress* situations, you would be increasing your ability to discuss the effects of *stress*, first with yourself, and with a professional counselor if it should be required.

We must recognize that usually, we are reacting to several *stress* situations at the same time. This would require that we determine the total amount of SRE being used up as we react to combinations of *stresses* in our daily lives. This could be accomplished by direct addition of the values we have assigned to the individual *stress* experiences. If we acknowledge that positive experiences would nullify negative ones, we would note that SRE values for negative experiences would be added together. Then SRE values for positive experiences would be subtracted from the total to produce the net amount of SRE for any particular combination of experiences that would be considered. For example, a negative marital situation, especially one generated by the partner's financial position, would experience a reduction in SRE units, if one spouse were to be given a promotion and increase in salary. Practice and sincerity in your evaluations are the criteria that would lead to a meaningful, reliable and successful exercise in assessing your reaction to *stress* and your abilities to remain below your **SREL** while under particular *stress* situation.

Once you have completed measurements (by way of the bias-free scale) for the more recent events in your life, you could turn your attention to past *stress* experiences. As you attempt the retroactive measurements, you may have to question some of the current values you have assigned to particular situations. This might require adjustments to the values chosen for your current experiences, or in the values being considered for the previous experiences. If you find the need to make adjustments, you should also consider your life style situations during the periods that you experienced particular *stress* situations, as life style management would be a contributing factor to one's ability to react to *stress*. Because we are all individuals, there is no set formula that could be employed to make adjustments for chosen life-styles however, over time you could develop personal expertise in the level of adjustments that may be required.

These general recommendations should permit individuals to begin the process of measuring the levels of their reactions to *stresses* in terms of SRE units employed. Some may be able to complete the evaluations by themselves. Others may require the assistance of a Counselor or medical professional, or someone familiar with the process, such as a friend or family member, who might have employed the process, successfully in their own life.

Any initial problems with using the bias-free measuring scale, should disappear after it has been used for a short while. The length of time it would take for a person to become comfortable with use of the scale would depend on the individual. Some persons might have to receive an extended period of guidance to reach a comfort level.

There is one caution regarding the selection of the scale to be used for your personal bias-free evaluation of your reaction to *stress*. Once you have selected a scale (1 to 10), (1 to 1000), or (1 to 1,000,000) you should continue with the same scale for all your measurements. **You should not attempt to add values from different scales to produce an SRE value for combined *stress* experiences,**

You should always remember that there are no correct or wrong values for any individual's reaction levels to *stress* experiences. However, understanding how you react at an individual level, and being able to assign numerical values to your reactions should assist us in understanding the limits of our abilities for dealing with particular *stress* situations. It would permit us to take a pro-active approach in maintaining balance in our lives (homeostasis), so that we would not, unknowingly, be propelled into distress that could wreak havoc with our lives.

Similarities and differences between the views of Dr. Selye, and the author

In his book, "Stress without Distress", Dr. Selye describes *stress* as the "non-specific response of the body to any demand made upon it." This definition indicates that human response is considered to be the *stress*. This definition differs from the author's, where the situation or event producing the demand is considered to indicate a *stress level.* The human response to the level of *stress* is considered as being reflected in the amount of re-adaptation energy effort required to re-establish the body's balanced condition while experiencing *stress.*

Dr. Selye also explains that each demand made on our bodies is unique or specific. He tells us that exposure to cold results in the specific response of shivering to produce more heat and contraction of the blood vessels in our skin to diminish the heat loss from the body surface. If we are exposed to heat, we sweat because evaporation of perspiration from the surface of our skin has a cooling effect. However, he points out that the derangement in our bodies in response to any kind of *stress* increases a demand for re-adjustment. These statements from Dr. Selye tend to be in agreement with the author's concept of a proportional relationship between *stress* and *stress* re-adjustment energy. He further states that the demand is non-specific, "...it requires adaptation to a problem irrespective of what the problem may be." He says that the "non-specific demand for activity as such is the essence of stress."

Dr. Selye and the author do not disagree significantly; however, the author believes that the demand for activity (re-adaptation energy) is the human response to *stress,* and not the *stress* itself. We could consider a debt "load" to produce financial *stress* for an individual. Then we would note that it is only when repayment of the debt becomes a problem that there would be any significant mental or physical evidence of *stress* observed in the body, or in the actions of the individual.

From his definitions and explanations, Dr. Selye appears to consider the intensity of the demand for readjustment to be the indicator of *stress*. However, unless the demand were always, to remain proportional to the *stress*-producing event, it could not indicate the level of *stress* being experienced. However, this inability to measure the level of *stress* would be understandable if the *stress* had already progressed beyond the **SREL** of the individual. It would also be unlikely that individuals would be able to obtain laboratory readings of the intensity of their non-specific responses to *stress* during their normal daily routines. However, people experience physical feelings and emotions as they experience *stress.* The development of a technique for utilizing interpretations of emotions and physical effects during periods of *stress* would be more practical and useful to individuals. The author uses his suggested response ratings for adaptation to *stress* in order to provide an indicator of human reaction to *stress.* This indicator would be more useful on an every day basis, than knowledge of the biological and chemical changes in our bodies that occur at some level of *stress* that is being experienced.

Engineering theory considers the internal reaction of materials (strain) to be produced by external loads that produce stress. Because we are able to obtain accurate measurements that indicate the relationship between stress and strain, we have a pro-active system that could predict behavior of materials, and which permits us to guard against exposure of materials parts to over-stress situations. A pro-active approach to human *stress* would suggest that a better understanding of the levels of *stress* that we experience under different stimuli and within different environments might be more useful for our lives. The author is suggesting that individuals could train themselves, or be trained to observe and record their reactions to *stress* by paying attention to comfort levels, changes in disposition and general feelings of good or poor health at the time that the *stress,* or *stress* combinations are affecting their lives. This type of information would serve individuals in the same manner that the engineers' knowledge of materials reaction to external stress serves to prevent over loading and possible failure.

Dr. Selye points out that, "It is difficult to see how such essentially different things as cold, heat, drugs, hormones, sorrow and joy could provoke an identical biochemical reaction in the body." He indicates that it has taken medicine a long time to accept the existence of such a stereotyped response. Individuals are exposed to different levels of heat, cold, hormones and prescribed medications therefore it is conceivable that, actually, he agrees that the response of each individual would vary. For some certain levels of cold, heat, sadness or joy might not provoke any discernible *stress*, but once a noticeable *stress* reaction occurs, we could anticipate a similar type behavior in the human body. The author believes that the essentially different things would all produce similar *distress* at certain levels. It is the similar *distress* states that are seen to produce the stereotyped response in the body. If the author is correct, then the situation that Dr. Selye calls stress is really *distress.* If the author is correct, then it should not be a surprise that the human body produces a stereotyped reaction for the same condition—*distress.*

Whether Dr. Selye is correct, or if the author is correct, the common denominator of identical biochemical reaction still would not tell us much about our abilities to, successfully, withstand any particular type or level of *stress,* or combinations of *stresses.* Dr. Selye acknowledges the fact of a variety of *stress* influences in our lives. This is evident in his statement, "Similarly, no matter what you do or what happens to you, there arises a demand for the necessary energy required to maintain life, to resist aggression and to adapt to constantly changing external influences. Even while fully relaxed and asleep, you are under some stress." If Dr. Selye is correct in this statement—which the author believes he is—then since *stress* is present when you are asleep and fully relaxed, the biochemical response should occur and there should be an alarm stage as depicted in his chart to explain the General Adaptation Syndrome. If the author is correct in his assertion that the GAS is only triggered after a *distress* condition exists, then the individual who is asleep and fully relaxed could be experiencing *stress* at a level that would not trigger the biochemical response in the body. Exceptions would be situations where the sleep condition might be disturbed by subconscious thoughts about different conditions or experiences, or where dreams create conditions that produce a high level of *stress* that might demand corresponding high levels of re-adjustment energy.

Dr. Selye advances a concept of a living organism, which is termed *"milieu interieur"* by which the organism has a need to remain constant despite changes in its external environment. He presents the argument that, "In order to maintain a healthy life, nothing within me must be allowed to deviate from the norm. If anything does, I will become sick or even die." The author believes that the adaptability of humans, of which Dr. Selye also speaks, would protect humans from deviations from the norm, unless the deviations were so great that normal and reserve re-adaptation energy would be insufficient to re-establish a balanced condition in the body. I believe that Dr. Selye saw things as he did, because what he considered to be stress was already excessive *stress* or *distress.* This would have meant that the individual was closer to a failure state than at the early stages of *stress* reaction.

Materials begin reacting to stress immediately as the stress effect begins to take place. However, each material possesses a built-in ability to resist stress because of its elastic properties. The author believes that the human body also has an innate ability to resist *stress.* There is no alarm reaction in materials if the stress being resisted is below the proportional limit. The author considers the human body to have similar abilities, as would be evidenced by the different levels of discomfort that would occur based on the different level of *stress* that might be experienced.

When we consider the actual *stress* situation that applies to human life, it would appear that many of the daily *stresses* we experience successfully are routine. They would be easily handled unless other situations that exist at the same time complicate our re-adaptation energy resources in a manner that affects our abilities to handle the routine occurrences. The routine events, although they may require re-adjustment energy, according to the author, would not, necessarily, take us beyond our SREL, and we probably would not trigger the biochemical response.

Dr. Selye is correct when he states that "stress plays some role in the development of every disease; its effects—for better or worse—are added to the specific changes characteristic of the disease itself." But he also points out that the effect of *stress* may be curative such as shock therapy and physical therapy. However, if the GAS consideration is correct, the condition of any *stress,* which is added to the existing *stress* resulting from some illness should always create a more critical situation for the individual.

If we consider human reaction to *stress* to be similar to the reaction of materials, it would appear that the introduction of "curative" *stresses* such as shock therapy would represent counteracting *stresses* to that produced by the illness. A simple analogy, in the case of materials, would be a situation where a material would be experiencing a harmful "tensile" (stretching) stress, but is prevented from experiencing failure by the deliberate introduction of a load situation that produces a counteractive "compressive" (pushing) stress.

We could assume that when *stress* in the human body reaches the point of *distress*, the body's need to rely on biochemical adaptation to resist the *distress* would affect the body's ability to deal with some of the routine situations we experience every day. It is the myriad of combinations of *stress* influences that the mind and body must cope with each and every day that is critical for the human condition. It is possible that the human body could withstand any single *stressful* experience, if it were possible to isolate that experience and cause the body to focus on that one condition. This might explain the different tolerance levels for individuals in dealing with the same *stressful* situations. Some individuals could walk on hot coals or beds of broken glass without experiencing pain or signs of excessive *stress.* Some people could train their bodies to withstand high levels of pain without experiencing significant discomfort. These things might be possible because of an individual's ability to concentrate re-adaptation energy to deal with individual, critical *stress* experiences. Dr. Selye seems to agree with the author's assessment in his book, "Stress without Distress". He writes the following: "In other words, the laws of self-preservation, as exemplified by the chemical feedback mechanism regulating resistance to non-specific stress (and even to some specific agent), are inherent in the sub-cellular structure of all living organisms and, hence, furnish natural guidelines for behavior in daily life."

Dr. Selye's comments appear to relate to Dr. Taylor Hartman's idea of basic personality traits. These traits could be related to the inherent chemical feedback mechanisms that regulate resistance to non-specific *stress.* Dr. Selye's comments also appear to be in agreement with the author's ideas about a proportional relationship up to the point of the normal stage of resistance identified by Dr. Selye, which the author describes as the Stress -Readjustment Energy Limit (SREL).

In the final analysis, the author believes much of Dr. Selye's work appears to reinforce the idea that we could analyze human *stress* reaction in a similar manner to the analysis of stress in materials.

Some closing thoughts about human *stress*

While it is possible to examine human *stress* by using a technique similar to the examination of stress and strain in materials, it is impossible to develop fixed *stress* limits for individuals. We can physically measure stress in materials, and we can test materials to the actual point of failure. We are, unfortunately, unable to do this with humans. Even if it were possible to sacrifice an individual human by causing the person to be *stressed to the point of ultimate failure (death)*, the information obtained would be useless for application to people in general, because we are each different individuals, who would require individual *stress* investigation. In addition to the individual nature of each human, the fact that the types and levels of *stress* combinations would be different for everyone would not produce beneficial results. The situation would be further complicated because our individual identities would permit each of us to react differently to the *stresses* we experience.

It is the individual nature of humans that makes general, arbitrary rating scales that assign a fixed number of points to certain *stress*-causing events or situations unreliable as *stress* indicators for determining the medical state of individuals. While loss of a spouse might be the most critical negative *stress* for one individual, it might be a positive *stress* reliever for another. If the person who dies was a spouse abuser, or if the spouses lived in a society where polygamy is permitted, the effects of the death of a spouse would be different. The same would be true if the spouses existed in a culture where death is clothed in a mantle of glory. For some individuals, the challenge of managing and building a business empire could be considered more important than marriage and family, and would determine the greatest *stress* that the individual might experience.

The importance and values that individuals assign to personal wants, needs and feelings would, probably always determine the extent to which individuals would be *stressed* by events and situations that impact upon those wants, needs and motives. Our physical and mental nature, as well as our innate personality types (as suggested by Dr. Hartman), would determine our capabilities to adapt, successfully, to the *stresses* we experience in our lives. Management of our lifestyles would lead to feelings of wellness, but it would not protect us from *stressful* events in our lives. We should realize that the *stressful* experiences, themselves, are not the problem. It is only when the experiences take us to a point where our normal and reserve re-adjustment energy is incapable of producing the re-alignment to return our bodies to the balanced states that we have become accustomed to, that we risk serious, permanent and possibly fatal results from *stress*.

Dr. Selye, and Dr. Hanson (the author of "Joy of Stress"), both suggest that we could control the *stresses* in our lives by controlling our choices. But controlling our choices of family environment, spouses and jobs are much easier to talk and write about, than they could be controlled in actual life situations. Because we are all individuals with different levels of financial security, intelligence and physical capabilities, the kinds of choices to permit the kind of wellness and *stress*-avoiding life styles would not be readily available to all of us. However, for those of us, who are financially and intellectually secure, it could take a simple event like a stock market crash to expose the fickle nature of relying on one's ability to choose, as a defense against negative *stress* situations.

Importance of lifestyle management in resisting *stress*

Lifestyle management at any level of existence in society contributes to our wellness and our ability to resist *stress*. It assists us in adaptation to re-establish homeostasis because a healthy mind and body require less SRE to deal with *stressful* situations. A body whose poor health and mental state causes imbalance that forces an individual to employ re-adjustment energy for homeostasis may not allow the individual to retain a sufficient amount of SRE for dealing with other *stress*-producing events that require use of adjustment energy.

We must also recognize that individual dispositions and lifestyle management produce *stress* influences of their own that could be taxing on re-adjustment energy. It is important that we do not generalize about human resistance to *stress*, or human wellness during *stress*, on the basis of the examples of the lives of particular individuals. One instance where this type of generalization is made without complete justification appears in the book, "Joy of Stress", concerning the late, Sir Winston Churchill.

Dr. Hanson, as does Dr. Selye, directly links *stress* and death. Dr. Hanson suggests that, "Life spans are shortened in groups that do not appear to have much control over their stress...." He also states that, "the biggest cause of illness and, ultimately, death is *mismanagement* (which is a polite word for *incompetence*)." He concludes that Sir Winston Churchill lived to the age of ninety in spite of smoking, drinking and obesity because of his constitution and "the effects of constant stimulation with stresses." Dr. Hanson also suggests that Churchill's "resistance to stress was also bolstered by a loving relationship with his wife, and the ability to take efficient cat-naps." But was it really stimulation by *stresses* that produced longevity for Winston Churchill? Are we to assume that by forcing ourselves to experience *stress*, we might be able to improve our longevity?

Perhaps Sir Winston Churchill was the right personality, at the right place, at the right time. Perhaps he was of the correct disposition and personality color code to deal with the type of *stresses* that his position and the challenges of war created for him. Perhaps Winston Churchill was the type of individual who could train his mind to concentrate on what he considered to be important and critical *stressful* situations, while blocking out the other *stress*-producing events that were occurring in his life at the same time. Winston Churchill was an individual with individual strengths and weaknesses, and individual ability to deal with the *stresses* he experienced at that particular time of his life. His particular circumstances might well be the recipe for others with similar personality code and "charactered" choices, but his situation should not be advanced as a general suggestion to indicate that experiencing high *stress* levels would produce longevity for others. This is the kind of error that occurs when we treat cases of *stress* to be the same for everyone. We could note that in his book, Dr. Hanson suggests moderation in eating habits and calorie counting as positive practices for wellness. He also indicates that smoking and excessive drinking are bad habits for the achievement of wellness.

Human *stress* failure

Experiencing *stress* without being *distressed* is an important message for all of us. However, we should recognize that we are not all able to choose the type of *stress* or the time it occurs in our lives. For some people, such as weightlifters and other athletes, excessive *stress* is used as a conditioning factor to keep them ready and capable of performing at a maximum level for competitive purposes. This process in an athlete's training is similar to the materials sciences process called "strain-hardening", which improves a material's ability to withstand imposed external stress. In the human body, we could experience extreme *stress* as long as it does not deplete our stress-readjustment energy capability. However, there are levels of *stress* that would not produce the ultimate failure, but which would cause other forms of human failure.

There is a suggestion in Dr. Selye's book that excessive *stress* and the expiration of adaptation energy to resist it would lead to death. This might be the case if the *stress* is of a medical nature. It might also be the result if sorrow and self pity leads an individual to become less caring of self to the extent that one's physical and health needs are ignored, which could lead to eventual death. However, I believe that, like materials, which exhibit failure in different ways, failure in humans, as a result of excessive *stress,* could be exhibited in ways other than death.

Failure in humans could take the form of denial that could cause an individual to avoid trying to succeed. Failure in the face of excessive debt could result in bankruptcy (although this could be a form of success in certain cases), or by an individual resorting to theft. The individual may resort to borrowing from a "loan shark" thereby creating a worse debt situation because of the high interest penalties. Resorting to gambling might also be an example of failure in a debt *stress* situation. The type of failure an individual exhibits under *stress* would probably be related to the person's character and the personality color code that motivates and directs the individual.

Some individuals are unable to cope with the *stress* of writing exams. Failure for these individuals could take the form of "dropping out", or attempts to cheat on exams. Individuals who succumb to the *stress* of married life could exhibit failure through divorce, extramarital affairs or abusive behavior towards spouses and children. People who cannot cope with the *stresses* in their lives could resort to suicides, or to drunkenness, drug use, or other activities that indicate failure.

We all die at some time, but often we might fail long before we die. There are a myriad of ways in which people exhibit failure in response to any number of *stress*-producing influences. Politicians exhibit failure from the *stress* of politics in many ways. Children succumb to parental and other authority *stresses* by leaving home, or adopting bad habits, or by giving up on their education pursuits. Groups, businesses and other ventures exhibit failure in many ways. Death of resolve is failure, and death is not always failure.

Method of *stress* reaction measurement suggested is not perfect

Individual *stress* experiences belong to individuals and to groups separately. Even if the *stresses*, or combinations of *stresses* are the same, and occur at the same time, individual abilities and individual responses to the events would always be different. Unless, and until we know which *stresses* and the levels of these *stresses* we could withstand, either singularly, or in combinations, we would not be able to engage in the correct choices that produce effective life style management and wellness for humans.

No perfect method is yet available to produce the kind of *stress vs. stress* reaction information for humans, which is available for engineers and materials scientists. However, the technique offered in this book recognizes the importance of individual reaction and provides a format for recording individual responses based on individual interpretation of the manner in which different *stress* situations affect individuals and groups.

Since each individual relies on personal interpretation of the effects produced in the person's emotional, mental, social, financial, physical and other states, it provides a better opportunity for individual discovery of personal reaction to *stress*. This should result in a healthier and more informative process that would lead to pro-active approaches to guard against experiencing destructive *distress* in our lives.

The success in interpretation of human reaction to *stress*, that would result from the use of the author's bias-free measurement chart might never equal the success achieved in predicting stress capabilities of materials. However, careful and conscientious use of the technique should help to make us more alert to our strengths and weaknesses in dealing with *stress* situations. The technique might help us to move out of the jungle, "in which our sense of values have become entangled and obscured." This would be in keeping with the wish of the late Dr. Hans Selye.

Why re-adjustment energy

A body that is experiencing *stress* is always adapting in order to cope. This adaptation does not bring the body back to a previous state of homeostasis; instead it produces a balanced state for experiencing the *stressful* experience, which would be a state that is different from the one that existed prior to the imposition of the *stress*. This new balanced state may not be the preferred one for the individual. However, I believe the individual would always prefer a balanced state that satisfies the person's motives, wants and needs. I also believe the natural inclination would be to seek to re-establish the preferred state, hence ***Stress Re-adjustment Energy*** **(SRE)**.

We do not adjust a *stress* we develop means to cope with it, and to eventually combat it. These means require an output of energy or internal fortitude. My choice of *Stress Re-adjustment Energy* (**SRE**) is not based on scientific examination, or explanation. It could have been termed *stress fighting energy, or stress balancing energy, or something else.* I trust the reader would accept my term of **SRE**, to define the use of energy in reaction to external *stress* in order to re-establish preferred states of existence during *stressful* times.

When we are experiencing *stress*, the body will make adjustments to allow us to continue our lives despite the presence of *stress*. However, the body would always try to return to its desired balanced state. It is this desire that is believed to direct us to readjust our bodily systems—hence *stress* readjustment energy.

Calvin K. Preddie

Appendices

Appendix 1

Terms Used In This Book

An explanation of terms used in this book might be helpful for identifying similarities or differences with terms used by Dr. Selye and others. In some cases, terms associated with Dr. Selye, or stated by the author are identified.

Adaptation Energy – humans (Dr. Selye)

Energy depicted by biochemical responses as the human body attempts to re-establish its balanced condition.

Distress – humans (Preddie)

Negative effects resulting from an individual's failing attempt at dealing with a stress; or from experiencing excessive or prolonged stress.

Elastic Limit – materials

Stress level at which a material experiences a deformation that cannot be reversed (permanent set).

Elastic Region – materials

The region on the stress vs. strain curve that identifies where a proportional relationship exists between applied stress and the strain reaction. If an applied, external stress is removed before a material reaches its proportional limit, the material returns to its original dimensions and retains its original strength capabilities.

Failure – humans

The point at which death occurs *(Dr. Selye)*

The point at which individuals become permanently incapacitated either physically, mentally or emotionally; or exhibits irrational, unethical, unhealthy or excessively emotional behavior. In some cases death occurs. ***(Preddie)***

Homeostasis – humans (Dr. Selye)

The relatively stable state, or equilibrium of interdependent bodily systems.

Natural Stress Re-adjustment Energy (SRE) – humans (Preddie)

An undetermined amount of energy that is available to each individual for use in the body's reaction to stresses.

Normal Level of Resistance – humans (Dr. Selye)

Level above which the stage of resistance occurs as depicted in Dr. Selye's G.A.S. chart. "Note that the author (Preddie) believes that the human body begins its resistance to stress, at the start of any stress event.

Natural Re-adjustment Energy Region—humans (Preddie)

The region, on the stress vs. re-adjustment energy curve, where there is a proportional relationship between stress and human reaction.

Proportional Limit – materials

The maximum stress level at which the relationship between stress and strain changes from a proportional one. It is similar to the SREL for humans.

Stress Re-adjustment Energy Limit (SREL) – humans (Preddie)

The maximum amount of SRE the body could expend in response to stress, prior to the utilization of reserve energy resources that are available to each individual. This limit is similar to the Proportional Limit for materials, and up to this point, the relationship between stress and stress re-adjustment energy is considered proportional. It would also be similar to the normal resistance level of DR. Selye's G.A.S.

Reserve stress re-adjustment energy—humans (Preddie)

This would be similar to the term adaptation energy as used by Dr. Selye. (Note that the author (Preddie) believes that adaptation begins at the onset of stress).

Reserve re-adjustment energy region – humans (Preddie)

A region shown on the author's curve of stress vs. stress readjustment energy, where reserve energy is employed because of the human desire to perpetuate life. The author considers this region, as one where heightened anxiety results in higher levels of biochemical changes. It would be the region where human "scarring" occurs, such as fear of a stress.

Rupture, or Failure – materials

An observable condition that demonstrates material failure that is demonstrated by a complete loss of ability to bear a load, and the building or structure would collapse.

Strain – materials

A technical term which describes the observable changes in dimensions of a material part when it is subjected to external loads. It is calculated by dividing the change in length by the original length before the load is applied.

Stress – humans

Corresponds to "strain" in materials (Dr. Selye).

Anything that changes the balanced state of the human body (Preddie)

Stress – materials

A technical term which describes applied pressure caused by load forces on materials. It is calculated by dividing the load by the cross-section of the material that is supporting the load.

Stressor, or Stressor Agent – humans (Dr. Selye)

A term that corresponds to the term "stress" from the materials sciences (Dr.Selye).

Ultimate Stress—materials

Maximum stress level a material can withstand before failure occurs. Actual level of stress at failure could be less than the ultimate because some materials have ability to retain some strength after maximum stress level is reached.

Appendix 2

A comparison of Three Stress Curves

In this Appendix, we will examine the typical stress vs. strain curve of the materials sciences (Page 122), Dr. Selye's General Adaptation Syndrome (G.A.S.) curve and the author's curve of stress vs. stress re-adjustment energy. In one diagram, Dr. Selye's G.A.S. curve will be reproduced and superimposed on the author's curve to highlight the regions of similarity. A comparison of these two curves would indicate a part of the reason for the author's contention that Dr. Selye was actually discussing distress under the term stress.

Materials Sciences Stress vs, Strain Curve

In the materials sciences stress vs. strain curve, you would see an inclined line from zero to a point called the "Elastic Limit". This is a region in which the stress produced by external loads remains proportional to the strain resistance in the material. It is also the region where, if a load is removed before the material is stressed beyond its "Elastic Limit", the material stress is returned to zero and the strength capabilities of the material returns to 100% of the original ability of the material to resist stress.

This principle could be understood by considering the reaction of an elastic band that is subjected to pulling forces applied by the fingers of two hands. As the material is pulled, it stretches and there is a noticeable extension in length; and if you look carefully, you would also see a reduction in the width of the elastic band as well. If you were to stop pulling on the elastic band, it would return to the original size, and you could pull on it again. Even though you are not being asked to measure the length of the extension of the elastic band, you would be able to notice that the greater force applied when pulling on it, the length of the stretch of the elastic band increases. You could continue to increase the pulling force on the elastic band for a while, but not indefinitely. Eventually you would reach a point where the elastic band becomes limp, and even though you could stretch it a little more, it would not return to the original state. If you should continue to increase the pulling force, eventually the elastic band would snap because it would have reached the point of failure. (Please do not carry out this experiment to the point of failure because you would probably be rewarded with stinging [burning] sensation when the elastic band hits your hand).

It is this region where the line on the graph is straight, but inclined, that is of pivotal interest to the engineers and materials scientists. This is the region where stress and strain is proportional, and the author is convinced that humans react in a similar manner. Knowledge of the existence of the proportional relationship permits engineers to design material parts that would not be stressed beyond the region where proportionality exists. It is also the region on the author's graph for humans that he considers to be neglected in the existing work on human reaction to stress. **"We should note that in engineering, we also use the strength properties of materials that continue to exist beyond the "Elastic Limit" in a manner of design termed "Ultimate Stress Design" to provide for the use of smaller size members to resist external stresses. Adequate safety factors are applied to permit this type of design; however a discussion of this method of design is beyond the scope of this book).** A comparison of this type of design with the author's curve could be made because the author contends that humans are capable of utilizing reserve SRE to resist the effects of stress that take them beyond their SREL.

Engineers react pro-actively to protect materials from exposure to excessive stress. The author is proposing that scientists and medical practitioners, and others should promote pro-active efforts by humans to reduce the possibility of being made to endure excessive or possibly crippling stress. The bias-free stress- reaction measurement scale is the method the author recommends for preventative action by humans to avoid excessive stress that could easily become distress.

In the typical stress vs. strain curve, you would note that rupture (failure) occurs at a lower level of stress than the ultimate amount of stress that the material could withstand. This only means that after a material has reached the limit of its strain resistance capabilities, a lesser amount of external stress could produce the final rupture, where the material would break apart.

The following diagram gives the Author's representation of the typical stress versus strain curve of the materials sciences.

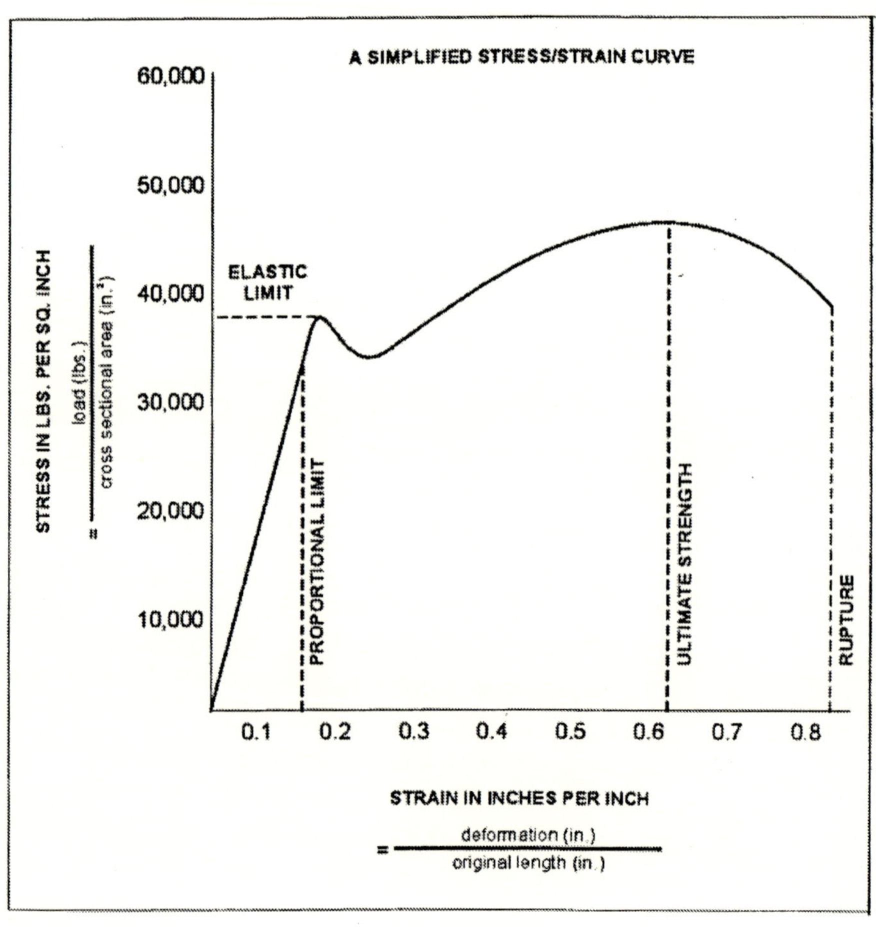

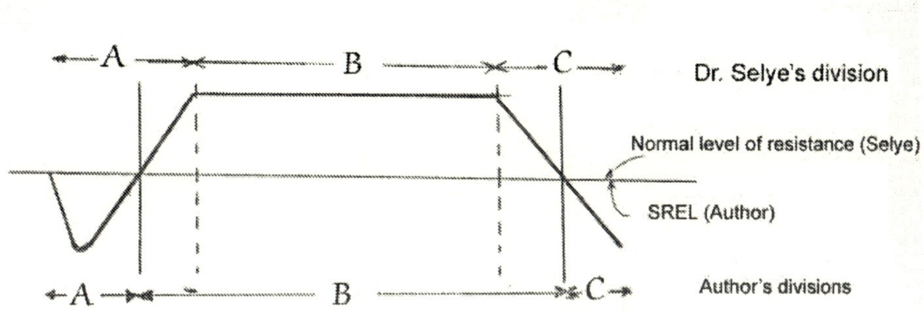

The diagram above is the Author's version of Dr. Selye's GAS (General Adaptation Syndrome) Diagram from his book, Stress without distress (pg 27) with the Author's ideas superimposed. Dr. Selye's GAS diagram is defined by the horizontal line denoting the Normal level of Resistance, the broken vertical lines and the solid line that extends from region A through to region C.

The solid vertical lines indicate the separation that matches the Author's concept of SRE (Stress Readjustment Energy) that is utilized by humans in resisting stresses being experienced. The broken vertical lines used by Dr. Selye explain his stages of human reaction to stress that are identified in areas A, B and C.

Dr. Selye calls Region A the Alarm Reaction. He states that at this time, "the body shows the changes characteristic of the first exposure to a stressor" and he says that, "At the same time, its resistance is diminished and if the stressor is sufficiently strong (severe burns, extremes of temperature) death may result."

The Author believes that during the initial exposure to a stressor (stress causing situation) the body might be unprepared to resist the stressor and requires time to put out the compensating amount of SRE to re-establish a balanced state, but the body's ability to resist the stressor is not diminished even though the level of resistance appears below the normal level.

Dr. Selye calls Region B the stage of resistance during which he states, "Resistance ensues if continued exposure to the stressor is compatible with adaptation The bodily signs characteristic of the alarm reaction have virtually disappeared and resistance rises above the normal."

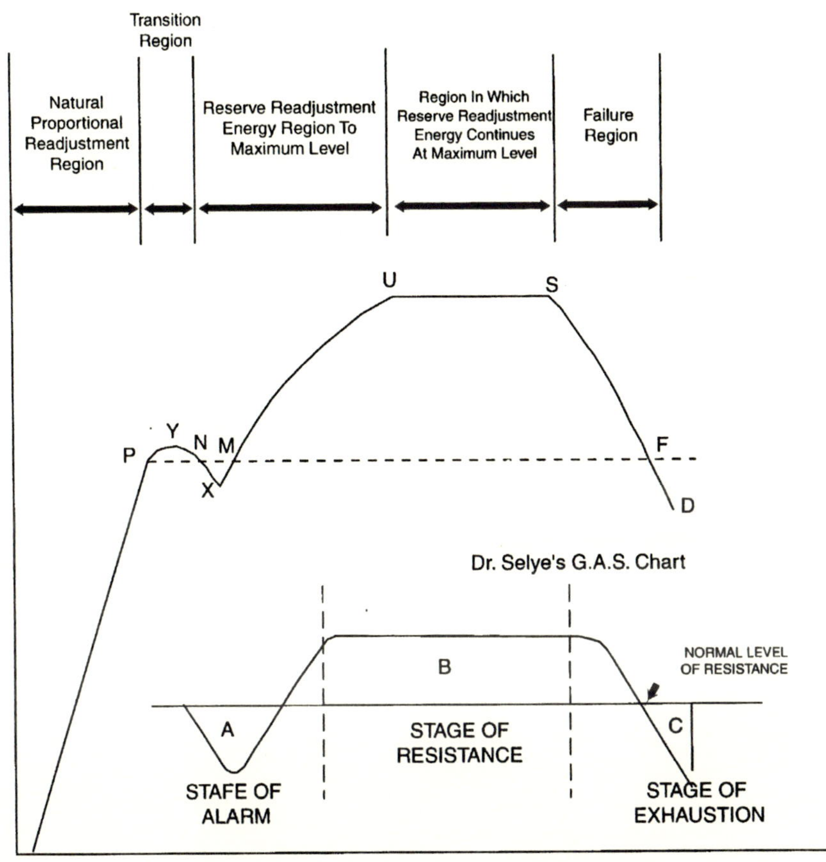

The diagram above shows the author's curve of stressor vs stress readjustment energy with Dr. Seye's General Adaptation Chart inserted for comparison.

The apparent similarity between Dr. Selye's Chart and the portion of the author's curve shown by region (NXMUSFD) stands out on the combnined diagram.

The apparent similarity helps to convince the author that Dr. Selye interpreted excessive stress, or distress to be what he referred to as stress.

Calpre CE Enterprises ®

The Author's stage B begins to the left of position of stage B in Dr. Selye's diagram and describes a region where the SRE is no longer proportional to the stressor and where reserve SRE is being utilized.

Dr. Selye calls Region C the stage of Exhaustion and contends that "...eventually adaptation energy is exhausted.The signs of the alarm reaction reappear, but now they are irreversible, and the individual dies."

The Author's stage C begins to the right of the comparable location on Dr. Selye's diagram. While this stage represents one where death might, finally, occur the Author believes that failure to be able to deal with a stressor does not always result in death. Failure could be evidenced in other ways such as alcoholism, irresponsible sexual activity and other forms of mal-adjustment in society.

A more detailed interpretation of Dr. Selye's GAS diagram and the Author's stressor versus stress readjustment energy curve follows in Appendix 3.

The author's curve has already been explained in a previous chapter. At that time, it was noted that three regions identified as, "A", "B" and "C" on the author's curve were shown for a later comparison with Dr. Selye's GAS curve. In this appendix, Dr. Selye's GAS curve is first shown separately, then superimposed on the author" curve from page 79. The similarity between region NXMUSFD on the author" curve, and Dr. Selye" GAS curve should be readily observable.

Except for the Proportional Region of the stress vs. strain curve for materials, and the similar Natural Proportional re-adjustment Region of the author's curve, there is no real difference between Dr. Selye's GAS curve and region NXMUFSD of the author's curve. Dr. Selye uses straight lines to go from the stage of alarm region A to the maximum level of resistance that is depicted by a horizontal line. The author uses a curved line to go from the Transition Region of his curve to the level of maximum Stress Re-Adjustment Energy Level at U. From point U, the author continues with a straight line to the point S, before dropping off with a curved line to the end point at D.

The author uses curved lines because by assuming a non-proportional relationship between stress *and* stress *re-adjustment energy in this region, a straight line would not, sufficiently, describe the relationship. Dr. Selye's use of straight lines to describe the change from one level to another suggests a proportional relationship, which might suggest a controllable situation where the GAS displays proportional increases and decreases with the imposed stress. The author also considers it unlikely that the decline from the maximum level of response to the end of Dr. Selye's curve could occur in a proportional manner, because the individual's ability to resist* stress *and to adapt would be failing rapidly.*

The similarity between Dr. Selye's three stages GAS curve, and the author's curve beyong the region of a proportional relationship between stress *and* stress *re-adjustment energy, helps to convince the author that Dr. Selye is really referring to excessive* stress *or* distress *when he discusses stress.*

Appendix 3

Charting Individual Stress Reaction Graphs

There are two types of graphs that could be developed with the bias-free stress rating scale. One could develop the relationship between levels of a particular type of stress *and the reaction of the individual, based on the definitions of the 10 different scales given for the bias-free rating. The other graph could chart the levels selected for various types of stresses, which would demonstrate the kinds of* stresses *that affect you the most. You could also use the graphs of the levels of particular types of* stresses *to determine a combined level for several types of* stresses *that may be affecting you at the same time. However, this third type of use would require the use of scale with values much higher than 1 to 10, for it to be useful to most people. Some examples are shown in the following pages.*

Sample Chart #1

Example Chart #1 shows a graph of stress *type vs. energy response rating level. The* stress *with the lowest energy response rating is debt under $1000.00. The other ratings shown are for family* stress, *which is not defined (there may be other types of family* stresses *that could be rated higher); and several other* stress *situations. The situations shown in this example range from severe illness, marital problems and a failed job interview to home mortgage default; however, there is an extensive list of* stress *situations that could be included in this type of chart. Each individual would have to work with the types of* stresses *that they could identify and for which they could assign a value on the chart.*

It would take some time for you to become familiar with the use of the graphs, and there are considerations that should be given to particular situations before you select a position on the graph that best represents your response rating level. In the example chart (#1), marital stress *is given the fourth higher level, just below job* stress. *However, if the marital situation happens to result from a minor dispute, such as disagreement about who should use the bathroom first when both spouses have to leave the house around the same time, it could suggest that the level of response chosen is too high for a situation that appears to be generated by a minor issue. It could mean that the individual is extremely sensitive to pleasing the spouse, which causes a trivial type of marital* stress *that would, normally, be trivial to many persons to create a high* stress *level for that individual. It could also mean that the existence of other* stresses *has combined with the individual trivial* stress *to produce a high level of combined* stress *for the individual. It is possible that some other event that could be related to the spousal situation causes the marital* stress *level of the individual to be increased. It could be a situation where the individual failed to obtain a job promotion that he/she had convinced the spouse to be a certainty. Apprehension about discussing the situation with the spouse for fear of a major disagreement could trigger an elevated* stress *level. It is vital that we examine our situations to determine the events that might have been occurring in our lives around the time that the particular* stress *is being evaluated for the level chosen. We may never be able to identify every thing that was going on in our lives at any time in the past, however, we should make the attempt to recall as much of the past as possible. There is a good chance that if you do not remember a situation, it might not have been very demanding of your* stress *reaction energy.*

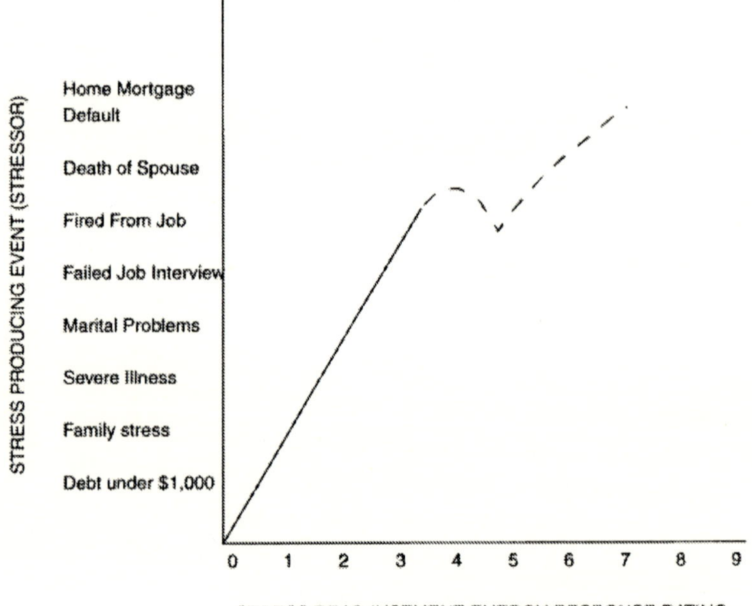

CHART 1: GRAPH OF STRESSOR TYPE VS RESPONSE RATING

Calpre CE Enterprises ®

From Chart #1, we should also note that the stress *of severe illness is listed as a less troublesome situation than marital* stress. *This could mean that the individual might have a relatively good resistance to the* stress *produced from medical illness.*

There would never be a guarantee that the stresses *listed have been correctly evaluated by individuals, nor would there be a guarantee about the levels we select on the charts. However, the effort to think about our situations when we are required to respond to various types and levels, and combinations of* stresses, *would provide us with important knowledge of our perceptions to situations in our lives. In most instances, our perceptions are the realities to which we react.*

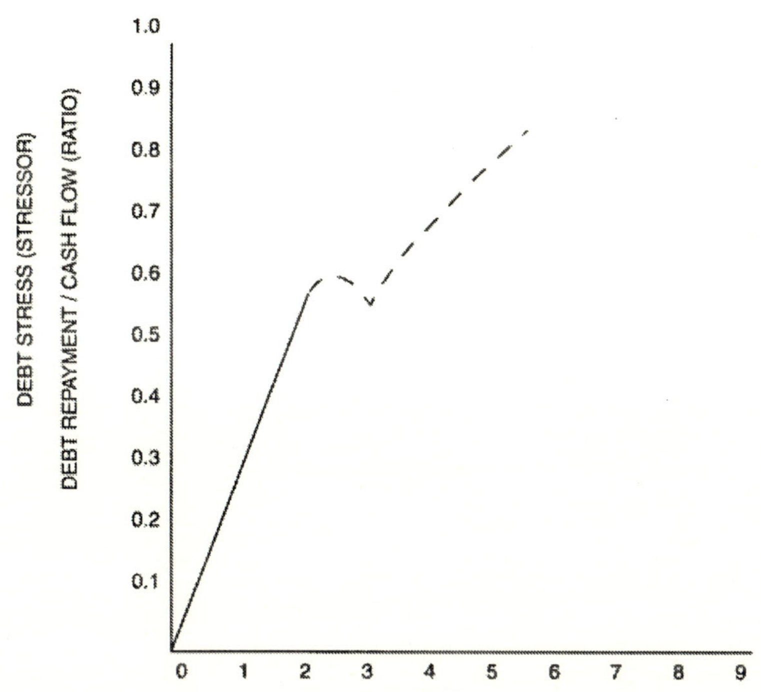

CHART 2: GRAPH OF STRESSOR LEVEL VS RESPONSE RATING

Example Chart #2

Example chart #2 plots debt stresses *vs. energy response ratings based on a set of debt ratios that indicate the ratio of debt to cash flow. Cash flow is considered to be the amount of money available to be spent after major monthly expenses are taken care of. Mortgage payments or rent payments, car payments or car lease payments, and other payments such as for insurance or fixed retirement funds deposits are considered to be major expenses. This type of graph could be utilized to apprise an individual about the level of debt that could be experienced without severe economic hardship that could produce detrimental* stress *situations.*

Example Chart #3

Example chart #3 is similar to chart #2. It plots different types of illnesses against levels of energy response ratings. The chart demonstrates that different types of illnesses would require different levels of energy reaction. The chart does not suggest that the order chosen for the example would be the same for each individual. Each individual would have to decide which type of illness creates the level of discomfort, from both the emotional and physical states, that is represented by the level of energy response reaction that has been chosen.

Example chart #3 might suggest that the individual is more susceptible to the pain of tendinitis than to the discomfort of an ulcer situation. However, as previously indicated, it is important to identify whether other stress *conditions were occurring concurrently with any of the illnesses for which levels are indicated on the chart. It is also possible that a case of tendinitis of the shoulder that would cause an individual to back out of a tennis tournament that was considered important would produce greater* stress *that would require a greater response reaction for certain individuals.*

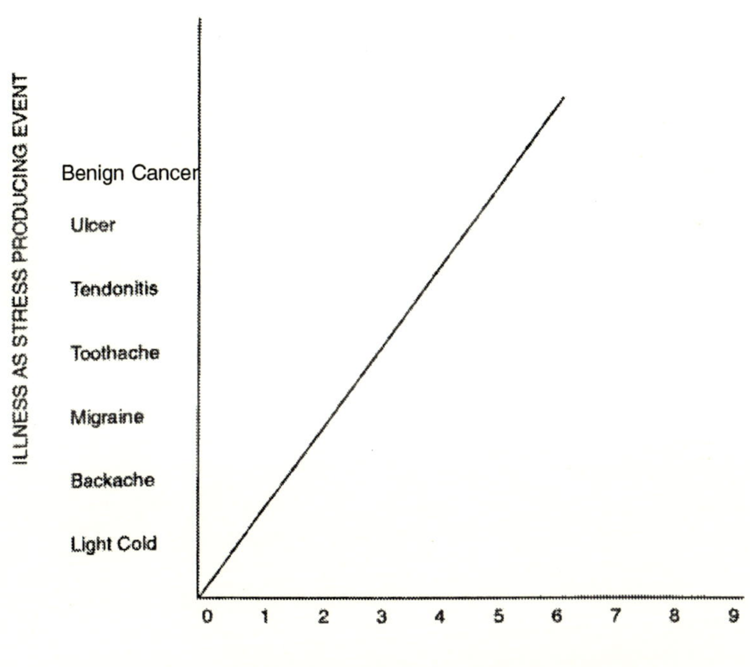

CHART 3 GRAPH OF DIFFERENT ILLNESSES VS RESPONSE RATING

Calpre CE Enterprises ®

Chart #4

Example chart #4 demonstrates graphs that are similar to the graph in example #1. This graph is intended to indicate that different individuals (A, B and C) might react differently to different stress-*producing influences. This type of variance is in keeping with the concept of individual reaction to* stress *and to combinations of* stresses. *The chart is simplified to indicate the effects of individual reactions; however it would be more complex in real life. Individual might actually be stronger in experiencing the death of a parent, and weaker in experiencing the loss of a job than individual B. Individual B might be stronger than individual A in a bankruptcy situation, but weaker than individual C when serious illness is to be considered.*

Because the charts are dependent on individual interpretation of feelings, emotions and physical and mental capabilities, one individual's chart could not be compared, meaningfully, with the chart of another. However, comparison of debt-ratio charts for different individuals could indicate the level of debt stress *that would affect a particular individual more than some other. In any event, the debt ratios would be determined on different money amounts, which would maintain the individual nature of the situation.*

Use of response rating charts with professional counselors

This manner or measurement of stress-*readjustment energy response to* stresses *that we experience in life is not ideal, and it does not carry the reliability of materials sciences measurements. However, when we visit professionals to assist us with our reactions to* stress *problems, they are forced to rely on our own interpretations of feelings and emotions in order to prescribe cures for us and help us to adopt proper physical and mental approaches to improve our health. In using this technique, individuals are actually applying the same skills that would be used with medical practitioners.*

If an individual is honest about feelings and reactions when preparing stress *response rating charts, the results would contain the same type of, and probably more reliable accuracy than the verbal responses made to questions of medical personnel and professional counselors when seeking care of one's body and the betterment of individual life. In any event, use of these charts would provide each of us with a better knowledge of self and the ways in which we may be affected by* stress. *It should also assist us to make pro-active decisions concerning our need to obtain professional assistance for dealing with the* stresses *that we must face in life.*

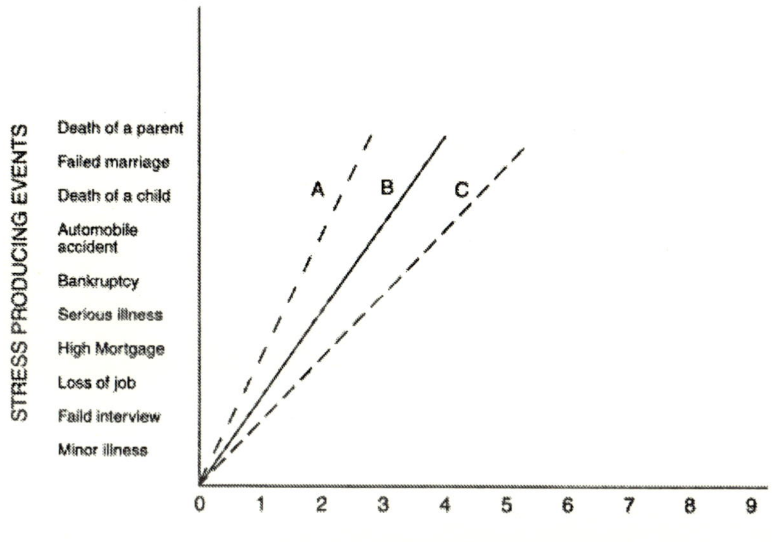

CHART 4: GRAPH OF STRESSOR TYPE VS RESPONSE RATING FOR THREE (3) DIFFERENT INDIVIDUALS A,B, AND C

Dr. Selye's G.A.S. Curve

In Dr. Selye's curve representing the General Adaptation Syndrome, he shows a stage "A". In this region he demonstrates an "Alarm Reaction". If this stage exists anytime an individual experiences stress, *it would suggest that any type or level of* stress *produces some initial exhaustion. The initial exhaustion, according to the G.A.S. curve, produces an alarm stage, during which human resistance begins to decline to a low point, before the body is able to provide resistance that would take the human system back to the normal resistance level in Region B.*

The concept of stress *producing an alarm reaction would appear to be certain when experiencing a new* stress *for the first time—such as a baby being required to exist on its own immediately after birth, or an Astronaut taking his/her first walk in space. However, having to experience a particular type of* stress *daily, should not produce the alarm reaction stage at each new occurrence, unless it is the type of stress that affects the person's physical state—such as illness.*

In Dr. Selye's curve, region A (stage of alarm) suggests that any form or level of stress *produces some initial exhaustion. The exhaustion leads to an alarm stage during which human resistance begins to decline to a low point, before the body is able to provide positive resistance that should take the human system back to the normal resistance level.*

According to Dr. Selye's G.A.S. curve, as the stress *continues, adaptation energy that is greater than the "normal level of resistance" (energy) then functions to produce a stage "B", which is called the stage of resistance during which the body successfully resists the effects of* stress. *The reserve energy is shown to increase (build) to a maximum level, at which it remains, until all the reserve adaptation energy is used up, and is followed by the third stage "C".*

In this third stage (stage of exhaustion), the level of resistance falls off to a point that is lower than the normal level of resistance and, in Dr. Selye's explanation, leads to the eventual death of the individual.

If what Dr. Selye calls stress, is really distress, *then the author is in general agreement with Dr. Selye's G.A.S. curve. However, the author does not agree that failure due to* stress *would always result in death. The author recognizes many types of failures that differ from individual, which occur before the ultimate and extreme failure of death. A crippling affliction; alcoholism; drug dependency; gambling, and non-social behavior are all considered to represent different types of failure because of excessive* stress. *However, the author would agree that once* stress *has advanced to the level of* distress, *if it continues, it would eventually lead to death. The author considers the effects of battle fatigue for soldiers to be a form of failure that results from* stress *(perhaps this is what is now referred to as Post Traumatic Stress syndrome). If* stress *were being produced by exposure to extreme cold temperatures, failure could take the form of fear that results in the individual leaving the inadequate shelter available and venturing out into the cold in search of being rescued, which could result in eventual death. The failure would have come before death.*

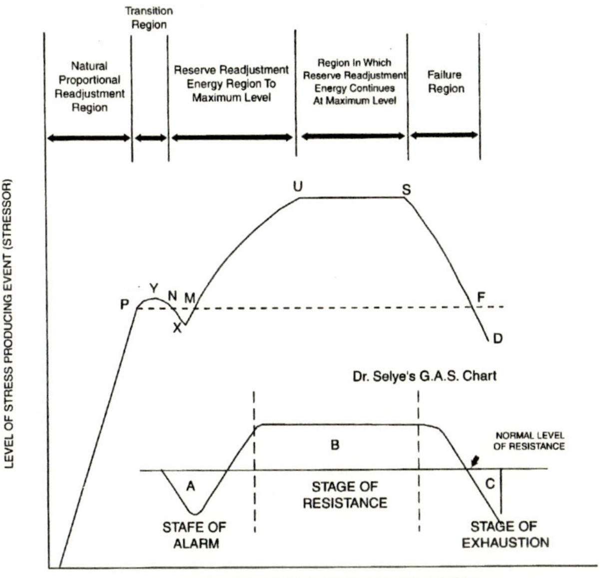

The diagram above shows the author's curve of stressor vs stress readjustment energy with Dr. Seye's General Adaptation Chart inserted for comparison.

The apparent similarity between Dr. Selye's Chart and the portion of the author's curve shown by region (NXMUSFD) stands out on the combnined diagram.

The apparent similarity helps to convince the author that Dr. Selye interpreted excessive stress, or distress to be what he referred to as stress.

Calpre CE Enterprises ®

***A interpretation of Dr. Selye's G.A.S. curve in comparison with the author's* stress vs. stress-readjustment energy curve.**

The author contends that Dr. Selye, and other stress *researchers and counselors are neglecting to examine* stress *before it becomes distress. It is the region where a proportional relationship exists that is being neglected in the treatment of the* stress *conditions of humans. This is the region that the author calls the Natural Proportional Re-adjustment Region, which is similar to the region that exists prior to the Proportional Limit point on the materials sciences stress vs. strain curve.*

Dr. Selye's curve indicates a "normal level of resistance". The author believes that such a level exists for humans. However, the author believes this level to be similar to the Proportional Limit level for materials. The author is convinced that the human body would react with a proportional amount of energy to establish balance in the human system. To do otherwise would cause an imbalance between a much greater response to a lesser need for energy to combat the effect of a minor stress *situation. Medicine appears to support the author through findings in the 1970's that if a* stress *is removed from the body stability returns. People do not perspire at the same rate or level every time the body needs to produce cooling temperatures. The amount of perspiration produced would be relative to the extent that the body needs to be cooled. Moderate exercise would not produce the same amount or rate of perspiration as extreme exercise activity. There is a limit to the amount of perspiration the body can normally produce on its own, and should the need for cooling temperatures persist, the body would continue producing at this maximum rate until some form of failure results.*

The curve on the author's graph is identified by the letters PYNXMUSFD. In the diagram where Dr. Selye's G.A.S. curve is shown below the author's, it is shown that Region "A" (stage of alarm) of Dr. Selye's curve is similar to the region NXM of the author's curve. Region MUSF of the author's curve is seen to be similar to Region "B" (stage of resistance) of Dr. Selye's curve; and region FD of the author's curve is similar to region "C" (stage of exhaustion) on the G.A.S. curve. The horizontal line PNMF of the author's curve is similar to the horizontal line on the G.A.S. that Dr. Selye considers to represent the "normal level of resistance".

Similarities exist between Dr. Selye's G.A.S. curve and the curve on the author's graph of stress vs, stress-re-adjustment energy, *beyond the region of a proportional relationship between* stress *and readjustment energy. These similarities produce the major reason that justifies the author's contention that what we now call* stress *is really an advanced state of* stress, *or distress.*

The author's curve shows a point "Y", which is similar to the "Yield Point" in materials which occurs at the "Elastic Limit" point as shown on the stress vs. strain graph for materials. It is at this point that the author considers extreme anxiety to affect the body which is at the limit of its natural ability to resist the stress *or combinations of* stresses. *The heightened anxiety produces an additional* stress *before the body can signal the need for additional re-adjustment energy to produce homeostasis, which weakens the body's ability to resist* stress *and results in the downward slope of the curve during the "transition period where ability to resist* stress *is reduced. This activity is shown to be similar to the activity depicted by the "stage of alarm region "A" of Dr. Selye's G.A.S. chart.*

If we examine Dr. Selye's chart, we would notice that he actually shows the stage of resistance to begin before the level of resistance returns to it's normal level. His "stage of resistance" region "B" depicts resistance above the normal level, but resistance had to be provided in stage "A" in order to return to the normal level. This situation is similar to the situation anticipated by the author, except for the fact that the author considers resistance to begin from the onset of the stress, *and to continue through to a point where failure occurs, or the* stress is removed. *Even after the resistance reaches its maximum value, the author believes it continues at a reduced rate until failure occurs. This pattern of continued resistance after the maximum level is also reflected in Dr. Selye's graph.*

The author is convinced that reserve re-adjustment energy is a reserve supply—such as the type of energy we refer to as a "second wind". Dr. Selye is considered to be correct, in his interpretation of the manner in which reserve adaptation energy (above the normal limit) is utilized to resist stress. *However, the author believes that Dr. Selye did not explore, completely, the concept of energy utilized to resist* stress *before became* distress *for the individual.*

Some additional thoughts about the author's curve

The author is convinced that, similar to inanimate material, humans react to stress *by producing an appropriate amount of re-adjustment energy to resist the experience through re-establishment of a balanced body condition (homeostasis). The proportional relationship up to the limit of normal re-adjustment energy is believed to be correct because overproduction of re-adjustment energy would, itself, produce an unbalanced state for the body. There might be situations where individuals could convince themselves that the* stress *has a greater effect than is true, and the body might be signaled to put out a disproportionate amount of re-adjustment energy. In these situations, as would also be the case if overconfidence caused the wrong signals which resulted in a lesser amount of re-adjustment energy than was required, there would be unbalanced body states that would require additional energy demands to create homeostasis.*

Subj:	(no subject)
Date:	1/15/2002 11:11:48 AM Eastern Standard Time
From:	merskey@on.aibn.com
To:	cpred22959@aol.com
Sent from the Internet (Details)	

Mr. Calvin Preddie

Dear Mr. Preddie:

Thank you for letting me have a look at your article. I appreciate the distinction you make between stress and strain. It has been known to me for a long time and I think it is a valuable comment, not often heard, because only engineers ordinarily know about it. On the whole I tend not to jump at opportunities to use structural models or similar conceptual approaches in psychological thinking. They have a good/bad history going as far back as Freud. Usually also there are difficulties in making analogies between the response of materials and the behaviour of people. On the other hand, your Stress Rating Scale recognizes some of the errors in the Holmes-Rahe Scale (which is really dropping out of use because it was inadequate for the complexities of the various situations).

In the end I can only offer you these scattered comments and am too heavily involved in some other issues to do any more on this topic but I appreciate having received your information and wish you well.

With kind regards.

Yours sincerely,
H. MERSKEY, D.M., F.R.C.P.(C)
/jd

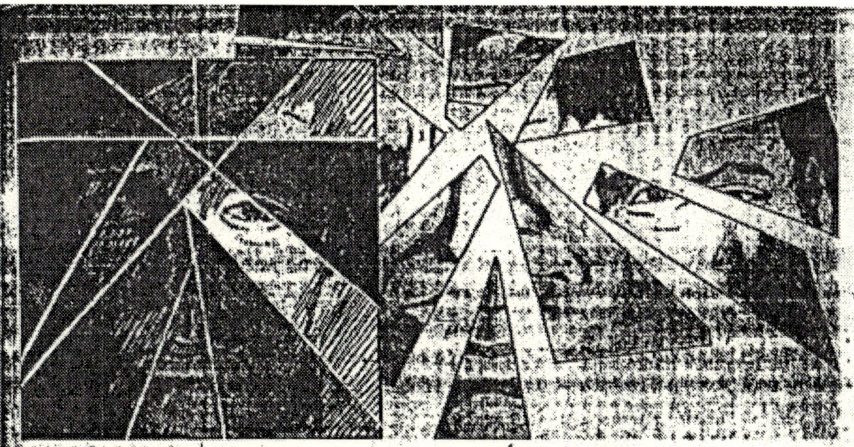

An Engineering Analysis of Man's Reaction to Stress

About the Author—Calvin K. Preddie, P.Eng., a graduate of Howard University, is a Teaching Master in Civil Technology at St. Lawrence College of Applied Arts and Technology, Cornwall, Ontario. Active in Association affairs, Mr. Preddie is currently Chairman, Eastern Chapter.

The Montreal Gazette of March 21, 1972, reported that Dr. Hans Selye, Montreal's world-famous expert on the biochemistry of stress reaction, had stated that *stress* causes violence today. He voiced the opinion that, "As a recipe for life, you should determine your natural stress level, the speed of life that fits you best. Then determine whether a certain problem is worth fighting for." What Dr. Selye recommends appears to have some similarity to efforts by engineers to determine stress levels for materials in order to safeguard against failures.

Other statements about human stress have appeared in the press in recent years. On June 1, 1970, a Montreal paper reported that a Rutgers University Political Scientist had cited a mass of experimental data to show that people make more mistakes while under *stress*.

The article suggested that *stress* produced aggressive behaviour in President Nixon and resulted in his decision to approve an attack on Cambodian soil.

Readers Digest, April 1972 issue carried an article entitled, "*Stress—Your Heart's Deadliest Enemy?*" From it, we learn that, "Impressive new evidence indicates that everyday tension and anger causes more coronary heart disease than all the traditional culprits—fatty foods, smoking, lack of exercise—combined."

Concern with the impact of *stress* on humans has grown steadily since the sole treatise published by Dr. Hans Selye in 1950—reportedly, there were close to 6,000 separate reports on stress research during 1971. Today's researchers have found a definite link between body chemistry and *stress*. They have also found that should a *stress* be removed from the body, stability returns, however, if the *stress* is prolonged, the body's defense system gradually wears down and deterioration follows.

In addition to the effects of occupational stress, the continually mushrooming world population and the accompanying growth of crowded cities have prompted many studies of the effects of life in a crowd. Researchers appear convinced that life in a crowd carries attending *stresses* that have a detrimental effect on our physical, social and sexual life.

Engineers' concern for the effects of stress has enabled them to devise safety factors to ensure that materials are not overstressed. Their analyses are governed by a theory of *Stress* and *Strain* with which almost all engineers are undoubtedly familiar. Engineers have determined for materials the stress levels that Dr. Selye recommends for human comfort.

Engineers are aware that the theory of stress and strain, develops the relationship between *stress* (load/cross-sectional area) and the resulting strain in the loaded material (elongation/original length). This relationship is known to be proportional up to a definite limiting value (proportional limit), which occurs prior to the material reaching its yield point (the point at which permanent deformation occurs). If a material is loaded beyond its Yield Point, it is possible that stress values may become high enough to produce rupture or failure of the material. At this point, the material loses its strength properties.

Some materials, such as steel are *elastic* (possess the ability to return from its deformed shape to its original form after an applied load is removed—this effect too, is possible only to a particular point, the *Elastic Limit*). There are special techniques (beyond the scope of this article) that could be utilized to produce in steel a greater capacity to withstand stress—provided it was not previously stressed beyond its Elastic Limit—so that upon a subsequent application of a *stress*-producing load, the *Proportional Limit* is reached at a higher stress value than that which was formerly required to bring about the disproportionate relationship between *stress* and *strain*.

Applying this theory to human life, we can visualize a person, during his life time, as being subjected to various types and amounts of *stress* which produces a *strain* response that represents his effort to cope with the *stress* being experienced. His *stress/strain* relationship is a proportional one until his moral, physical and psychological strength reaches a point where he will have to exert himself more to cope with minor increases in *stress* producing experiences. At this point, the individual is at his *Proportional Limit*, and should the stress producing stimuli persist, the individual could be stressed to a point where he is unable to function in a normal manner. The person is then at his *Rupture Point*.

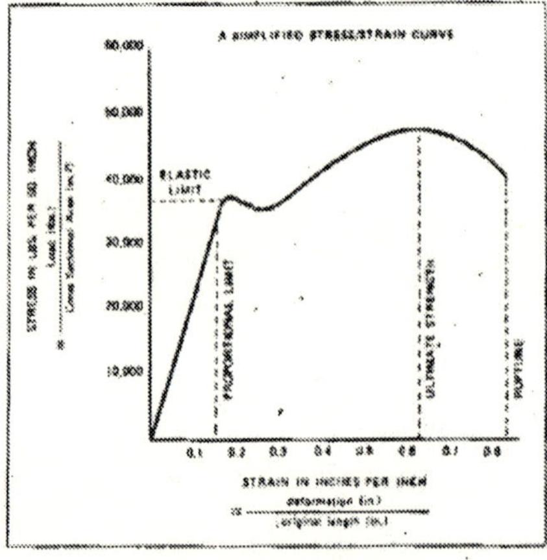

When a material reaches its *Rupture Point*, it might break, or buckle. It loses its strength properties. When an individual arrives at his *Rupture Point*, he is unable to control his actions and thoughts and is incapable of rational action, or physical efforts. He is no longer able to cope with the demands of life because the strength properties that previously sustained him (moral, physical, etc.) are lost. In modern terminology, he has "blown his cool", or is "wasted".

If we can accept the idea of man having a *Proportional Limit* and a *Rupture Point* that would be indicative of his reactions under conditions of *stress*, and if we consider him to possess the property of *Elasticity*, and we can further say that removal of the *stress* producing influences before he reaches his *Proportional Limit* would allow the individual to marshall all his strength to resist the *stress* if it were again forced upon him. Also, by the *Strain Hardening Process*, a man could actually exhibit increased strength properties that would render him better able to cope with similar stresses in the future.

The principle of *Strain Hardening* is realized in our daily lives, although we may be unaware of it. In training individuals, constant exposure is used to condition and prepare them for whatever activity is to be expected. In sports we have warm-up games and exposure to competition prior to the actual contest. Astronauts must complete a comprehensive and taxing training process in preparation for their tasks in space. Nature also relies upon a similar principle in preparing us to cope with life. Every experience conditions us for our roles in the future, and if an experience does not take us beyond our *Proportional Limit* initially, then we are better prepared to cope with stresses of life resulting from a similar experience in the future.

Two stress producing influences with which we are probably familiar are financial responsibilities and the perpetuation of good health.

Financial affairs affect every individual's life either directly or indirectly. A man in debt is under some form of financial stress as long as that debt, or a portion of the debt remains. In most cases, repayment of the debt is made in fixed installments that usually require some form of adjustment in personal finances because it represents a reduction in available spending money. This adjustment reflects our *strain* reaction, and when fixed monthly installments are considered, the proportional relationship between the financial *stress* and budgetary *strain* with which we respond can easily be visualized.

If a man is able to repay his debt within the stipulated time limit, his *stress/strain* relationship remains proportional throughout. However, if because of mounting living costs, or the indulgence in some unwarranted expenditure, the debt cannot be repaid on time, then the man is *stressed* beyond his *Proportional Limit*. Although the balance of the debt may be greatly reduced, the effort to complete repayment that forces the budgetary restrictions to be continued for a longer period represents the increased *strain* that would no longer be proportional to the amount of debt *stress* being experienced.

Creditors would not permit the debt to be carried forever, and the longer the period the man takes for repayment of the debt (which is amassing interest), the greater is the possibility that the individual could be stressed to his *Rupture Point*. Evidence that a man has reached this point of failure is found in his reactions at that point. He may resort to gambling or theft, and may even attempt suicide. Some men might plead bankruptcy. Others might place themselves in greater debt without realizing how the increased debt affects their financial stress.

However, if an individual is able to repay his debt on schedule, or if he is able to liquidate his debt prior to the set time limit, he will not be stressed to his *Proportional Limit* and he will continue to possess all the strength he requires to deal with further debt *stresses*. An important factor, is the reaction of the credit world to a man who repays his debt on time. This person's capacity to borrow is usually enhanced and he is generally considered good for an even larger loan. From an engineering standpoint, he has been *Strain Hardened.*

Declaring oneself bankrupt might appear to negate the argument of the *Rupture Point*, but the effects of bankruptcy could reduce a man's capacity to borrow. His strength properties could be severely impaired where borrowing money is concerned.

The wealthy are also susceptible to debt stresses. They may take the form of worrying about the nature of one's investment; or trying to devise ways to protect one's riches. We are aware of the accepted connection between businessmen and their ulcers and we know that emotional stress could lead to ulcers.

Financial institutions are aware of individual limitations where borrowing is concerned. They attempt to insure themselves and their customers against excessive debt stress by extensive checking through credit bureaus, and through credit counselling.

Applying a similar analysis to the experience of ill health, we observe that the human body experiences some form of aggravation from even a minor illness. It is possible for an individual to function efficiently despite the minor irritation of an illness, e.g. the common cold, but the fact that the illness does not impair a person's ability to perform only indicates that he is not stressed to his *Proportional Limit.*

There are times when an illness severely affects an individual's ability to function normally and his production suffers. Such a person has been stressed beyond his *Proportional Limit* as a result of his illness. If the illness continues, the person may be confined to bed, and in some cases may become incapacitated for life, and may even die.

Analyzing health stresses, we see that illness produces the *stress*. The physical and mental effort to cope with the sickness is the *strain* reaction, and when this effort impairs our ability to perform, or forces us to be bedridden, we have been stressed beyond our *Proportional Limit.* If the individual becomes permanently incapacitated, or dies, he has been stressed to his *Rupture Point.*

The *Strain Hardening* affect in the case of an illness can be best understood by the resistance the body develops to any form of disease once it has been successfully experienced previously. This is more apparent in the case of illnesses such as small pox or measles. We should note that the medical profession attempts to provide us with a system for guarding against excessive health stresses through the suggestion of periodic physical check-ups.

The *stress/strain* relationship is applicable to every area of life. It is relevant to the *stress* produced by driving a motor vehicle; studying; competition in any endeavour; coping with married life; coping with a society that stifles. In a group sense, it could be applied to the *stress* of racial conflict, and to the *stress* experienced by youth living in a world dominated by the wishes of adults.

When we attempt to discuss individuals as we would consider materials, we must realize that each individual represents a unique and different material. Different materials react differently to various types of *stress* and exhibit failure in different manners. For example, concrete is considered stronger than steel in compression, whilst steel is stronger in tension. The type of failure that may occur in any material may be due to *shear, buckling, deflection,* or some other type of failure.

Applying this trend of reasoning to man, we would note that individuals react differently to various types of problems, and that similar problems may produce different reactions in different individuals. Thus there are many ways in which failure may be evident in an individual, and the type and time required to produce failure under a particular type of stress would differ from individual to individual.

Some individuals may be able to withstand the *stresses* of financial burdens without being stressed beyond their *Proportional Limit,* but it is possible that these individuals would appear weak by comparison, when faced with the stresses produced by ill-health.

Others may react favourably to problems of ill-health, and succumb quite easily under the burden of financial stress. The differing reactions are similar to the different reactions of steel and concrete to tensile and compressive forces.

Two individuals subjected to the same type of debt stresses may both exhibit failure in the same manner—they may both resort to gambling—but the amount of debt necessary to cause one individual to gamble may be much smaller than the amount required to produce the same reaction in the other individual. This type of reaction is similar to the ability of materials to withstand certain stresses on the basis of the size of the structural members produced from the material.

In engineering, it is important to know the type and nature of failure that a given material will experience under different loading conditions. Materials can be studied, and their strength properties can be measured. Thus an engineer is able to pre-determine the reaction of a material when it is subjected to a particular type of stress, or combination of stresses. This information is vital if the engineer is to guard against failure of his works.

Unfortunately, in life such facilities are not yet available. However, it is conceivable that in the present computer age a system could be developed to chart *stress/strain* curves for individuals that could serve to appise them of their *strets* capacities and capabilities

If individuals could be made aware of their *stress* endurance levels, they should be capable of proper functioning in our society that should protect against irrational decisions and actions that seriously disrupt and affect our lives. Engineers have been able to establish *stress* levels for materials. Their methods could probably assist the human *stress* researchers at the Harold Brunn Institute at Mount Zion Hospital in San Francisco, USA.

Other areas in which Engineering analyses may be helpful in improving life are the mechanics of joint action; the hydraulic (pipe flow) analysis of the blood pumped through our veins and arteries; the structural analysis of our skeletal frame, and others.

Undoubtedly, more collaboration between doctors, people in social and psychological work and other scientists and engineers would prove extremely beneficial to men.

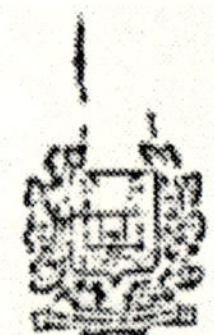

UNIVERSITÉ DE MONTRÉAL
Institut de medecine et de
chirurgie expérimentales

May 29th, 1972

Mr. Calvin K. Preddie
Teaching Master
Engineering Systems
ST. LAWRENCE COLLEGE OF APPLIED
ARTS & TECHNOLOGY
Cornwall Campus
Windmill Point
Cornwall, Ont.

Dear Mr. Preddie:

Your letter of May 11th with the enclosed manuscript arrived during my absence on a lecture tour in Europe but, immediately upon my return, I hasten to tell you that I read it with interest and profit.

Unfortunately, my competence in the field of engineering is insufficient to appraise the article from that point of view, but I am sure your comments will be of assistance to me in making comparisons between stress in animate and inanimate objects.

The only two minor comments I should like to make are:

1. In biology, we speak of stress in connection with what the engineer would call strain, whereas the engineer's concept of stress corresponds in medicine to "stressor agents".

2. My name is spelled "Selye" and not "Seyle". [p.s. I believe I transposed the (y) and (l) on the envelope] C.P.

I am returning your manuscript and would certainly appreciate it if you would send us reprints after the article appears.

Very sincerely yours,

Hans Selye

Hans Selye, C.C.

HS/rb:ln
Encl.

UNIVERSITÉ DE MONTRÉAL
Institut de médecine et de
chirurgie expérimentales

March 22, 1974

Mr. Calvin K. Preddie
816 Carleton Street
Cornwall, Ontario
X6H 4Y5

Dear Mr. Preddie:

It was very kind of you to send me a copy of your excellent article which appeared in Engineering Digest. I only received it this morning so I have merely glanced through it meanwhile, but I am sure I shall read it with much interest. It has arrived exactly at the right time as I have been asked to compose a "Stress Index" summarizing key publications on stress as applied to various disciplines, and I certainly will give yours adequate attention. Should you publish anything else along these lines in the future, please keep me up-to-date.

Very sincerely yours,

Hans Selye

Hans Selye, C.C.

HS/gd:jr

Case postale 6128, Montréal 101

Mount Zion Hospital and Medical Center

1600 Divisadero Street / San Francisco, California 94115 / Telephone (415) 567

May 19, 1972

Mr. Calvin K. Preddie
St. Lawrence College of Applied Arts
and Technology
Cornwall Campus
Windmill Point
Cornwall, Ontario, Canada

Dear Mr. Preddie:

I want to thank you for the very fascinating article which you were kind enough to send me, and which I enjoyed reading.

It is, of course, a fact that every individual has a breaking point. This is particularly well shown by the so-called nervous breakdown and by the battle fatigue exhibited by soldiers which in earlier days was erroneously termed shell-shock. It is far less recognized that a minor or moderate excess along these lines is certainly responsible for many mistakes in judgment. Most people only recognize the extremes such as actual breakdowns.

I found your analogy to stress and strain of building materials to be a particularly fascinating one, and you have certainly described this beautifully. I would urge you to submit this article to one of the psychological journals such as the Journal of Psychosomatic Research. It would certainly be instructive to all readers. It would also help us in the conception of our work here.

Sincerely yours,

Ray H. Rosenman, M. D.
Assistant Director
Harold Brunn Institute

RHR:ed

Printed in the United States
1197900005B/28-48